DEADLY DISEASES

NICK ARNOLD

illustrated by
TONY DE SAULLES

D1018067

SCHOLASTIC

Visit Nick Arnold at
www.nickarnold-website.com

Scholastic Children's Books,
Euston House, 24 Eversholt Street,
London, NW1 1DB, UK

A division of Scholastic Ltd
London ~ New York ~ Toronto ~ Sydney ~ Auckland
Mexico City ~ New Delhi ~ Hong Kong

First published in the UK by Scholastic Ltd, 2000
This edition published 2008

Text copyright © Nick Arnold, 2000
Illustrations © Tony De Saulles, 2000

ISBN 978 0439 94446 5

Printed and bound by CPI Group (UK) Ltd, Croydon, CR0 4YY

26

The right of Nick Arnold and Tony De Saulles to be identified as the author and
illustrator of this work respectively has been asserted by them in accordance with
the Copyright, Designs and Patents Act, 1988.

CONTENTS

I FEEL SICK, SIR, CAN I GO HOME?

Nick Arnold has been writing stories and books since he was a youngster, but never dreamt he'd find fame writing about deadly diseases. His research involved catching colds, grappling with germs and trying out plague cures and he enjoyed every minute of it.

When he's not delving into Horrible Science, he spends his spare time eating pizza, riding his bike and thinking up corny jokes (though not all at the same time).

Tony De Saulles picked up his crayons when he was still in nappies and has been doodling ever since. He takes Horrible Science very seriously and even agreed to draw malaria-carrying mosquitoes. Fortunately, he has made a full recovery.

When he's not out with his sketchpad, Tony likes to write poetry and play squash, though he hasn't written any poetry about squash yet.

INTRODUCTION

Are you well?

If so, GREAT. If not, maybe you need the *Horrible Science* treatment! Take one copy of this book and read it in large doses – after food. (Reading it before meals can ruin your appetite.) You're bound to feel better because laughter is a great healer!

(AND THAT'S JUST THE CONTENTS PAGE)

And if you're not ill you ought to read this book anyway to maintain a healthy sense of humour.

This book is especially effective against SLUMP disease (that's Science Lessons Upset Mystified Pupils). Sufferers of this common condition often slump over desks and feel a strong urge to sleep. And sadly, SLUMP disease can prove deadly … deadly boring, that is.

I'M BORED

I'M DEAD...

I'M ...EAD

INFECTIOUS PATHOGENS, BLAH BLAH, MUMBLE, DRONE.

Well, if you're a SLUMP sufferer, cheer up! This book contains medically proven ingredients such as sick jokes and sickening stories and seriously sick facts to fight SLUMP disease by boosting your brain power. This treatment is so successful that afterwards you can test your teacher and dumbfound your doctor with your deadly disease discoveries! Read about fiendishly foul phenomena like the nurse who drank diarrhoea…

…and the scientist who died of the disease he was studying…

…and the doctors who *killed* one another because they ar… …sease.

Feeling better yet? You will soon. Just keep on reading! But be warned…

SIDE EFFECTS OF THIS BOOK CAN INCLUDE SNORTS OF LAUGHTER AT EMBARRASSING MOMENTS, AND FEELING AN URGE TO TRY REVOLTING EXPERIMENTS.

Well, what are you waiting for…?

THE SICKENING FACTS

DISEASES COULD WIPE OUT THE HUMAN RACE!

It sounds sickening – but is it a fact? Well, you can check on your survival chances later on, but now it's time for a story to get your brain juices going…

THE INVASION

The aliens landed on a Saturday at about 7.30 pm.

Alex and his parents were having tea when they arrived. Huge dark green shapes loomed at the windows, lumbering like bears. There was a crash as an alien vaporized the door with its heat gun. It had two staring eyes like a giant squid and tentacles around its mouth.

"ARGGGH!" screamed Alex.

"Blimey!" said his dad.

"Hello, vicar," said his mum, searching for her glasses.

"Ulla ulla ulla!" said the alien, opening its razor-sharp fangs.

All three humans turned to run. There was a whooshing sound followed by a nasty burning smell as one of the aliens microwaved the cat.

Within hours the army had sealed off the area. The roads were clogged with people trying to flee. Everyone was unsure where to go, everyone was scared. It was worse than the first day at a new school.

"Don't panic!" shouted the general through a battered army megaphone. "We'll stop them!"

Just then a red haze appeared glowing against the sky. It was a cloud of gas billowing and tumbling like thick smoke. Ahead of the gas, soldiers from an advance patrol came running and stumbling and choking and falling.

"Gas masks!" ordered the general.

"Er … sorry, sir, we left them at the base!" stammered his sergeant.

"Then we'll have to make a rapid strategic withdrawal!" barked the general.

"Come again, sir?" asked the sergeant.

The general swung round bellowing "THAT MEANS RUN, YOU BLITHERING IDIOT!"

Soon the whole country was in uproar. All the roads were jammed with cars trying to escape the gas that hung in little wisps and unexpectedly seeped under doors. There was no TV because the aliens had knocked out the electricity system, but at least the schools were closed. Alex and his parents found themselves hiding in a sewer.

"I need some fresh air!" gasped Alex as he clambered towards the entrance.

"This living room needs a good clean," said his mum (who still hadn't found her glasses).

"You'll need more than fresh air if the gas gets you!" warned his dad, but the boy wasn't listening.

Alex sniffed the air. It seemed fresh enough. Well, it would after the sewer. So he decided it was safe to look for food and crept cautiously down the road. Suddenly he froze – an alien patrol had appeared round the corner! There was nowhere to hide. Alex closed his eyes and waited to be microwaved.

But the aliens ignored him.

They stumbled and shuffled past saying something like…

"Ulla, urgle, gurgle!"

Thick orange dribble slobbered from their mouths and their tentacles were droopy.

10

Taking courage, Alex followed the aliens into a field where he saw an awesome sight. Several spacecraft were leaning at drunken angles. All around lay aliens, many dead but a few twitching. There was a vile smell like rotting school-dinner cabbage.

The boy couldn't believe his eyes.

The aliens were sick, they were being destroyed.

But how and why?

Just then an alien sneezed a big glob of purple snot. Alex realized that the aliens had the most appalling, stinking colds. The invaders hadn't been defeated by the army or by anything that humans could do. No, they were beaten by humble common-or-garden germs.

Cool story?! It was inspired by a novel, *War of the Worlds* by H G Wells (1866–1946), in which diseases halt an alien invasion. Bet you never knew that hovering over every 6.4 square cm of ground there are 4,000 microbes looking for somewhere to land, someone to attack. And if you live in a big city there'll be about 400,000 germs hovering over your head! It's enough to make your hair curl.

No wonder the aliens never stood a chance!

So what about us? Are we going to be wiped out like the aliens? Well, germs certainly give us a tough time – you can be *dead* sure of that. But before we delve into their murky world – here's a chance to check your existing knowledge.

ODD DISEASES QUIZ

1 Which of these animals does NOT get colds?
a) Teachers.
b) Ferrets.
c) Fish.

2 Which of the following animals does NOT get flu?
a) Pigs.
b) Ducks.
c) Woodlice.

3 Which of the following treatments is USELESS against germs?
a) Feeding a maggot on diseased flesh.
b) Smearing a wound with honey.
c) Plonking a dollop of bat's poo on a wound.

4 Where will you NEVER find germs?
a) The moon.
b) Mars (that's the planet not the choccie bar).
c) A school dinner.

5 Which substance is USELESS for killing germs?
a) Moon dust.
b) Custard.
c) Toilet cleaner.

Answers: 1 c) If fish got colds their paper hankies would go soggy.

You may be interested to know that in the 1930s a scientist discovered that ferrets get colds after a ferret sneezed on him and he developed the illness.

2 c) Ever seen a woodlouse sipping lemsip?

In fact, you can catch flu from pigs and even ducks (that's when you need a quack doctor!). You can breathe these germs in or, even worse, the germs pass out of the animals' faeces (poo) into water. If humans drink the water we fall ill too. Sickening, eh?

3 c) The poo is crawling with germs. Doctors in Washington DC, in the USA, covered an injured girl's germ-infected leg with 1,500 maggots. The maggots ate the germs and diseased flesh but left the healthy bits. Honey is great for killing germs – the sugary stuff dries them out. That's why honey keeps for months in a cupboard after you've opened it. Mind you, if you want to keep your family sweet don't go smearing their honey on your scabby wounds and then putting the knife back in the pot.

4 b) Scientists tested Martian soil for germs in 1977 and found none. School dinners are full of germs and scientists have even found germs on the moon! In the 1970s astronauts brought back a piece of an old lunar-landing vehicle left on the moon in 1967. Inside the protective casing of the vehicle's camera, the scientists found germs from snot that had got into material when it was made. *The germs were still alive!*

5 b) Germs happily scoff custard. Toilet cleaner contains bleach, a highly effective germ-killer. And scientists in Houston, USA, have found that moon dust actually contains chemicals that kill germs – trouble is your local chemist probably doesn't sell moon dust and if they did it would cost £5 million a gram!

A NOTE TO THE READER

This is a little book about a big subject. There are thousands of different diseases. There are nasty diseases, smelly diseases and diseases you can't even tell your mum about. Some are caused by poisonous chemicals and others by worms in the guts. To fit them all in a book you'd need a book the size of a bookcase. So to save space, this book deals only with the deadly diseases caused by tiny living things – microbes.

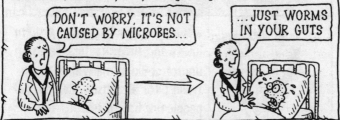

DON'T WORRY, IT'S NOT CAUSED BY MICROBES...

...JUST WORMS IN YOUR GUTS

So how are you feeling now? Maybe a bit shivery, or perhaps a bit sick? Perhaps these germs might be doing something nasty to *you*? Could it be that you've already got one of the deadly diseases we'll be looking at in this book?!

SHIVER!

SHAKE!

SWEAT!

TREMBLE!

We've hired Dr Grimgrave – the most miserable doctor in the world (he really ought to read a *Horrible Science* book to cheer himself up!) – to tell you the worst...

DR GRIMGRAVE'S GUIDE TO SYMPTOMS

So how are we today? Deadly disease, eh? Well, I'll need to examine you ... do you have any of these symptoms? If you aren't sure, I can arrange a consultation but not for idiots and time-wasters. Being a doctor could be enjoyable if it wasn't for all those whinging, sick people one has to see.

VIOLENT COUGH

Coughing is normal. I encourage my patients to cough into a handkerchief because it's the body's way of removing mucus

OFTEN A LOVELY GREEN COLOUR

(snot) caused by an infection. A violent cough, fever and huge lumps under the armpits and black spots on the skin may be a sign of one form of plague. Rapid burial in earth may be the most effective treatment here.

Dear reader

We apologise for the poor quality jokes. Dr Grimgrave is not known for his sense of humour.

16

DEADLY DIARRHOEA

Severe diarrhoea turns from brown to green and becomes paler when it contains the gut lining. This could be a sign of cholera. If untreated, there is continuous diarrhoea until the victim's body dries out. My old colleague, Dr Twinge caught cholera and he nearly dried of it.

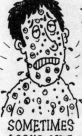

SOMETIMES LOOKS LIKE **BIGPOX**, HA HA!

PUS-FILLED PUSTULES

Spots are caused by minor infections resulting in a build-up of pus. Violent fever, muscle pains and spots filled with pus covering most of the upper body were a symptom of smallpox. In severe cases large chunks of flesh die and fall off the victim's body — most unhygienic.

DANGEROUS DRIBBLING

IT'S A MOUTH-WATERING EXPERIENCE!

Uncontrollable salivation can be a symptom of rabies. Other signs include fear of water, and an inability to swallow. By the time the disease reaches this stage there is no cure. Honestly, what do these patients expect me to do ... heal them?

17

BRIGHT YELLOW SKIN

The liver fails and chemicals escape and build up under the skin – jaundice, we doctors call it.

(I always think that if the liver is bad you should try onions – they improve the taste no end. Ha ha.) Jaundice and black vomit are signs of yellow fever. I have a sample of this remarkable regurgitation in my private medical collection.

FEEL LIKE DEATH AND *LOOK* LIKE A BANANA!

BLACK SICK

PLEASE NOTE: you're unlikely to have these deadly diseases. Most mild diseases can be treated by taking a painkiller and going to bed and allowing the body to heal itself. That way you don't bother me, your doctor. Now, if you'll excuse me, I've got work to do...

We'll be getting to grips with the gore and pus later on, but first a question: what actually *causes* all these deadly diseases? Yep, I'm sorry, but it's time to look at some deadly disease germs, and you can catch them in the next chapter...

GRUESOME GERMS

Take a peek down this microscope and you'll see them…

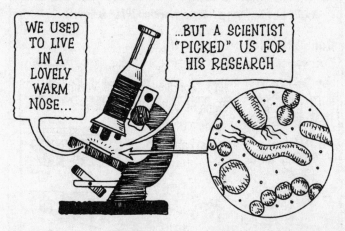

Not much to look at, maybe, but they're the nastiest and deadliest killers the human race has ever known. Just take a look at their files…

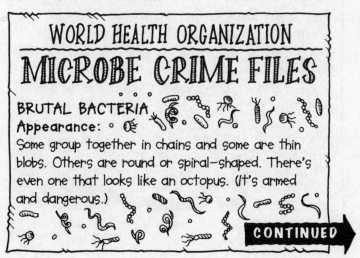

CONTINUED →

Size:

Most bacteria are 0.5 – 1.5 micrometres in size. (Up to 10,000 bacteria can stretch across your thumbnail – you'd better wash your hands afterwards!)

Horrible places they live:

Everywhere! Bacteria particularly like dirty places, like sewers or mounds of poo. Millions live in your guts (where they do no harm except make chemicals that make farts smelly).

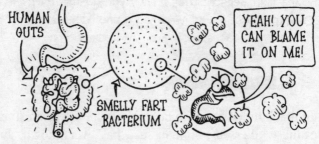

HUMAN GUTS

SMELLY FART BACTERIUM

YEAH! YOU CAN BLAME IT ON ME!

Favourite food:

They're not fussy. In fact, they even eat school dinners! They particularly like bits of dead or live body if they can get inside the skin. And many bacteria love human blood with its comforting warmth and delicious gloopy sugar snacks. (Luckily for the germs, there isn't *too* much sugar in blood, unlike honey!)

NIBBLE! SCOFF! YUMMY! DELICIOUS! S'NICE! SLURP! ERK! UGH! YUCK!

LIVE BODY   DEAD BODY   BLOOD   SCHOOL DINNER

Nasty habits:

Make deadly chemicals called toxins (tock—sins) that can stop human nerves working so the person can't move. The toxins kill by stopping the victim's breathing or disrupting their heartbeat. These bacteria are heart—less!

Brutal behaviour:

If they're warm and well—fed, bacteria happily increase in numbers by splitting in half. (Yeah — they're split personalities.) They can do this every 20 minutes, so in just nine hours one bacterium (one of these things is a bacterium, two or more are *bacteria*) can produce 100 million copies.

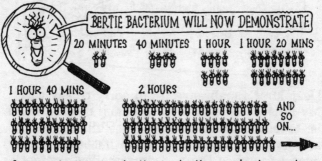

BERTIE BACTERIUM WILL NOW DEMONSTRATE

20 MINUTES   40 MINUTES   1 HOUR   1 HOUR 20 MINS

1 HOUR 40 MINS   2 HOURS   AND SO ON...

If they do this inside the body they make huge slimy lumps that break up the body's vital organs and cause death. Yikes!

TERRIBLE TB

By now you might be wondering what bacterial diseases are lurking in wait for you. The answer is *plenty*. For example, besides the plague and cholera, there's tuberculosis (ter-burk-u-lo-sis) or TB. Trust Dr Grimgrave to break the news gently…

HEALTH NEWS

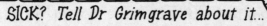

SICK? *Tell Dr Grimgrave about it...*

Dear Doc,
I have a slight fever and I'm coughing blood and loads of snotty phlegm (sorry about the stains). What's wrong with me?

I. Cannabreeve

Dear Mr Cannabreeve,
My hobby happens to be breeding bacteria and judging by the ones I found in the stains on the letter – you have TB.

I'm sorry to say that this lung disease is the biggest killer in the world but a course of drugs called antibiotics should save you.*
PS Don't call me Doc.

Your body is trying to clear your lungs of the Tuberculosis bacteria.

INFECTED LUNGS

* For more information on antibiotics see page 68.

Mind you, if you think that sounds bad – just wait until you see the next section of the MICROBE CRIME FILES.

MICROBE CRIME FILES ~ PART 2

VICIOUS VIRUSES

Appearance: Weird-looking – some are like lunar landing craft and others look like anti-ship mines covered in spikes.

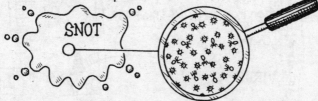

SNOT

Size: 17 to 300 nanometres. You could fit a chain of ten *million* viruses across your thumbnail (though you'll need a steady hand and a lot of patience).

ANTI-SHIP MINE

DEADLY

DEADLIER

VIRUS

Horrible places they live: Viruses have no proper bodies to protect them from heat or cold and that's why they live inside cells. (No, not *police* cells, silly, I mean the tiny living blobs of jelly that make up our bodies.)

Favourite food: Viruses don't eat or breathe. In fact, some scientists reckon they're not even alive! Think of viruses as vampires – creatures neither dead nor alive that prey on unsuspecting humans. No wonder they're a pain in the neck!

Nasty habits: The virus sticks to a cell and hijacks the control system of the cell and forces it to make copies of the virus. When the cell is worn out it dies and the viruses go in search of another victim. (For more details see page 111.)

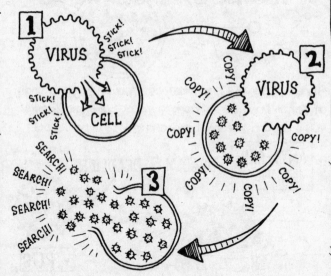

Vicious behaviour: Viruses often spread in tiny drops of spit that spray out of the mouth when we cough or sneeze. This danger is not to be sniffed at. Here are some interesting notes that I wrote on my hankie...

SNOTTY SNEEZY FACTS

1 One sneeze can contain *six million* viruses! Next time a cold makes you sneeze try counting them!

2 Millions of microscopic snot lumps shoot out of your nose and mouth at over 100 km per hour. If your sneeze was a gust of wind it would be strong enough to snap twigs off trees!

3 Within seconds the water in the snot dries out encasing the germs in hard dry snot-like tiny bullets (but too light for anyone to feel). If someone's in the way some snot might go down their throat or up their nose and some might go on their hands and they might then put their fingers in their mouth. And that's how your germs get into someone else.

WOULD YOU LIKE TO BORROW MY HANKIE?

NO THANKS!

MICROBE CRIME FILES - PART 3

REVOLTING IN-BETWEENIES

No, that isn't their scientific name. These are actually living things that are smaller than bacteria and bigger than viruses – the best known are rickettsia (rick-ket-see-a).

CONTINUED ▶

Appearance: Tiny blobs of colourless jelly.

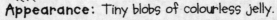

WIBBLE! WOBBLE! SLITHER! WRIGGLE!

Size: 0.5 micrometres across. You could fit 20,000 in a line across your thumbnail. (Now where did you put those viruses?)

WIBBLE! WOBBLE! WRIGGLE! SLITHER!

NOW YOU KNOW WHY MUM SAYS, "DON'T PICK YOUR NOSE!"

Horrible places they live: Rickettsia live inside insects like ticks and lice. Typhus rickettsia live inside blood-sucking lice that lurk on unwashed bodies. Maybe that's why they spread lousy diseases? The germs emerge in lice poo or eggs which enter the human body through the skin when it is scratched.

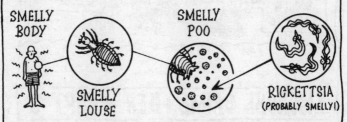

SMELLY BODY

SMELLY POO

SMELLY LOUSE

RICKETTSIA (PROBABLY SMELLY!)

Because the rickettsia are so small they can hide inside body cells and this makes them hard to find.

Nasty habits: Typhus rickettsia cause the disease typhus fever.

Bet you never knew!

The posh scientific name for typhus rickettsia is Rickettsia prowazeckii *(rick-ket-see-a prow-a-zecky). If this germ had friends they could always call it Ricky. It's named after American scientist Howard T Ricketts (1877–1910) who found the germ in 1909 and Stanilaus von Prowazeck (1875–1915) who studied it in 1915. And guess what? Both men caught typhus and died horribly. Well, looks like the germ discovered them too.*

SO WHAT IS TYPHUS FEVER?
Dr Grimgrave knows the dreadful details…

HEALTH NEWS

SICK? NEED ADVICE?
Write to Dr Grimgrave and if he's not too busy he might bother to reply to your questions…

Dear Dr Grimgrave,
The day before yesterday I had backache. Now I've got a splitting headache, fever and I think I'm starting with a rash. I can't sleep. Am I going to die?
        Yours,
                        Vera Sicke

Dear Ms Sicke,
Yes, probably. You have typhus and you may die of heart failure caused by germ toxins. But the rash might turn to sores which might rot and if your fingers and toes are infected they might drop off. If so, could you spare them for my private medical collection?

> IF YOU COULD SPARE FIVE FINGERS, THAT WOULD *REALLY* BE GIVING ME A HAND

If you want to get better, I'd recommend antibiotics, which should stop the disease developing.

Now if you'll excuse me, my patients are getting impatient.

> IF YOU CAN'T SLEEP TRY LYING ON THE EDGE OF THE BED ~ YOU'LL SOON DROP OFF

Now back to those files…

MICROBE CRIME FILES - PART 4

PUTRID PROTOZOA

Appearance: Blobs of colourless jelly. Protozoa look a bit like human cells and that makes them rather hard to spot inside the body. Imagine trying to find a toffee in a chocolate factory.

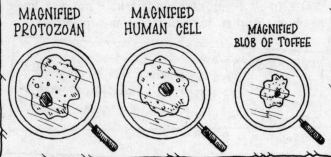

MAGNIFIED PROTOZOAN

MAGNIFIED HUMAN CELL

MAGNIFIED BLOB OF TOFFEE

Size: Most are less than 0.5 millimetres across. (So you'd need at least 20 big-uns to stretch across that grubby thumbnail.)

Horrible places they live: Often make themselves at home inside other creatures – in places such as guts or blood where they cause disease by making toxins.

Nasty habits: It depends on the disease. Take malaria for example – this disease is caused by protozoa with as much conscience as a gang of piranhas in a goldfish bowl.

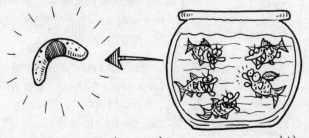

Deadly disease fact file

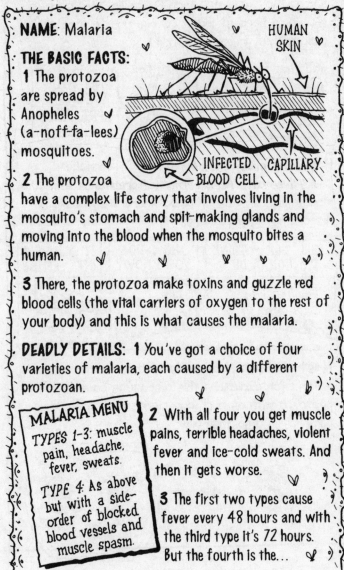

NAME: Malaria

THE BASIC FACTS:
1 The protozoa are spread by Anopheles (a-noff-fa-lees) mosquitoes.

HUMAN SKIN

INFECTED BLOOD CELL   CAPILLARY

2 The protozoa have a complex life story that involves living in the mosquito's stomach and spit-making glands and moving into the blood when the mosquito bites a human.

3 There, the protozoa make toxins and guzzle red blood cells (the vital carriers of oxygen to the rest of your body) and this is what causes the malaria.

DEADLY DETAILS: 1 You've got a choice of four varieties of malaria, each caused by a different protozoan.

> **MALARIA MENU**
> TYPES 1–3: muscle pain, headache, fever, sweats.
> TYPE 4: As above but with a side-order of blocked blood vessels and muscle spasm.

2 With all four you get muscle pains, terrible headaches, violent fever and ice-cold sweats. And then it gets worse.

3 The first two types cause fever every 48 hours and with the third type it's 72 hours. But the fourth is the...

4 REALLY nasty version. Around half the victims die as dead blood cells block blood vessels in the brain. Muscle spasms follow, so bad that the victims sometimes bite their tongues in half!

FINK I'FE GOK THE FORF HYPE!

Bet you never knew!
1 There have been germs – bacteria, viruses and protozoa – for millions of years. They're some of nature's great survivors – which is more than you can say for their victims. Scientists have found fossilized dinosaur bones that had been attacked by bacteria. I expect the dinosaur was an Ouchmybonesaresaur.
2 Every day you shed ten billion flakes of dead skin – they just drop off your body as fresh skin forms underneath. You can see a few of these bits if you turn a dirty pair of black trousers inside-out. At least two-thirds of these foul flakes carry bacteria and viruses.

3 So when you clean your room you stir up these bits and breathe in your own skin and germs!

COULD YOU BE A DOCTOR?

A patient has a boil on his nose. The boil is caused by bacteria and the red swelling is full of lovely golden pus.

Oh well, it could be worse – it could be a boil on the foot. Then you'd have pus in boots! Anyway, what forms this substance?

a) It's gas given out by the bacteria.
b) It's blood sucked in by the bacteria.
c) It's a mixture of dead blood cells and dead bacteria.

Answer: c) The blood cells died heroically fighting the bacteria.

Want the full story? It's in a top-secret deadly-disease-fighting document. And it just so happens we've got a copy and it's in the next chapter…

YOUR BATTLING BODY

Fancy a fight? Well, your body does. Every day it's spoiling for a fight – with germs! And here, as promised, is a unique glimpse of those top-secret military battle plans…

TOP SECRET DOCUMENT

KEEP OUT OF REACH OF MICROBES!

The Human Body Defence Plan

BY MAJOR GERM-BEATER

The body's defence mechanism, or "immune system" as we insiders call it, is based on phased defence and counter-attacks … so stand to attention for this important briefing!

MILITARY BASES AND ROADS

The defence system is based on military roads called the lymphatic (lim-fat-tic) system, complete with army checkpoints called lymph nodes, or "glands", where white blood cells re-group to fight infection.

33

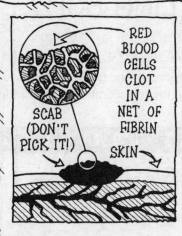

RED BLOOD CELLS CLOT IN A NET OF FIBRIN

SCAB (DON'T PICK IT!)

SKIN

LINES OF DEFENCE

1 Skin barrier

I'd like to see the germ who can burrow through this thick leathery wall! Trouble is, humans do insist on scraping or cutting their skin and allowing germs in.

2 The snot barrier

Known to us defence professionals as "mucus". The sticky snot of the nose or windpipe or guts bogs down attackers and contains a substance that kills some germs. Our front-line troops deployed here are the mast cells. They're under orders to release a chemical they store called histamine (his–ta–meen). This widens gaps between cells in blood vessel walls – allowing killer white blood cells (see opposite) to leave the blood and fight the invaders. Meanwhile, watery snot is released to flush out the enemy!

ARGH!

FLUSH THEM OUT!

ALL NOSE-PICKERS SHOULD BE COURT-MARTIALLED!

Some humans pick snot from their noses and eat it. This disgraceful habit allows germs caught in the mucus to enter into the guts where they can cause diarrhoea if not dissolved by acid in the stomach.

3 Bloody warfare

a) As a result of the gaps forming between cells, the blood vessels naturally get larger and more blood rushes to the area making it feel hot. That's why body parts, where there are germs, appear red and swollen.

b) Germs can die if they get too hot – so we aim to make 'em sweat by heating up the blood! White blood cells send chemical signals to the brain, which responds with chemicals that cause

the body's cells to make energy faster. This gives off extra heat. The skin turns pale as blood is retained deep within the body so it doesn't lose heat to the air. Humans call this "fever" – I call it a jolly good tactic!

All army units must counter-attack with every weapon at our disposal!

WHITE BLOOD CELL ARMY UNITS...

The T-cell army
T = top secret code for thymus (thi-mus) area where the army is recruited and trained.

This army is made up of three operational units...

THYMUS

1 The killer cells are combat personnel with orders to search out and destroy all germs. All body cells believed to be hiding germs are to be eliminated without mercy!

2 T-helper cells are highly trained intelligence and communications specialists. They identify germs and produce a chemical signal alerting the B-cell army (see opposite), and order the killer cells to move in.

3 T-suppressor officer corps'. Their job is to stop the others getting carried away and attacking in too great numbers. This could result in damage to the body as, inevitably, civilian body cells will get killed in the fighting. Yes, it's tough – but this is WAR!

THE B-CELL ARMY

B = top secret military code for
bone marrow training
centre where the army is
recruited and trained.

BONE MARROW

1 Each B-cell is trained to identify
enemy antigens. That's military jargon for any
invader of the body. ("Antigen" – just saying
that word makes me feel dirty!) Each B-cell is
covered with chemicals like tiny keys that lock
into chemicals on the outside of a particular
antigen. And since we have millions of different
B-cells there's every chance that for any antigen
we'll have a B-cell to fit it. You can rely on the
B-cell army to get to grips with the enemy.

2 Specialized B-cells are based in the lymph
node bases ready to make antibodies. If an

antigen is detected, the bone
marrow training centre will send
millions of B-cell reinforcements
with the right key to search out
antigens wherever they're hiding.

THE ANTIBODY WEAPON SYSTEM

These are guided missiles used by our troops to
lock on to antigens and destroy them. Each
antibody is designed to cover an antigen and
gum it up so it can be engulfed by the tank
corps (see next page).

37

WHITE BLOOD CELL TANK CORPS

Our tanks – we call them macrophages (mac-ro-fay-ges) – capture the gummed-up enemy bacteria by grabbing them in their mechanical arms and pulling them inside. All prisoners are to be dissolved alive! Remember – WAR IS NOT A TEA PARTY!

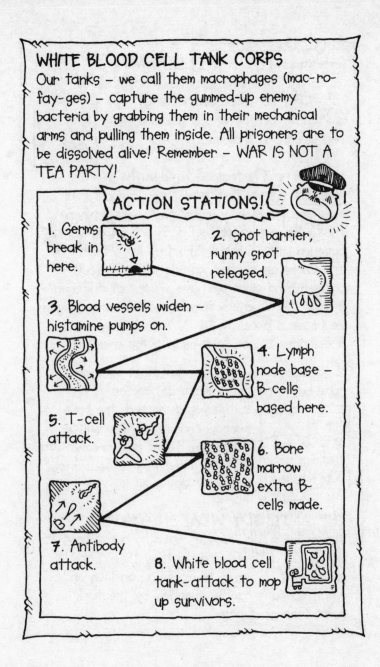

ACTION STATIONS!

1. Germs break in here.

2. Snot barrier, runny snot released.

3. Blood vessels widen – histamine pumps on.

4. Lymph node base – B-cells based here.

5. T-cell attack.

6. Bone marrow extra B-cells made.

7. Antibody attack.

8. White blood cell tank-attack to mop up survivors.

38

DEADLY EXPRESSIONS

A scientist says…

I'M INTO INTERFERON

Do you say…?

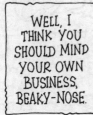

WELL, I THINK YOU SHOULD MIND YOUR OWN BUSINESS, BEAKY-NOSE.

Answer: He said "interferon", not *interfering*. All cells make interferon (in-ter-fear-ron) if attacked by viruses. It doesn't save them but in ways we don't understand this chemical stops the virus from multiplying.

Bet you never knew!
Your defences against disease can make you ill! Asthma sufferers are unusually sensitive to little bits of chemical like pollen from flowers or pollution from cars. When they're breathed in, the mast cells in the lungs that make histamine go into overdrive. And although this substance widens the blood vessels it actually narrows *airways and causes breathing problems. It's enough to make you gasp!*

You're probably an expert in what viruses can do to the human body. Yes, you are! If you've ever had a cold you'll know *exactly* how it feels. The bad news is that after hundreds of years of medical research even the cleverest doctors still can't cure a cold. The good news is that the body cures itself anyway. Here's how it's done…

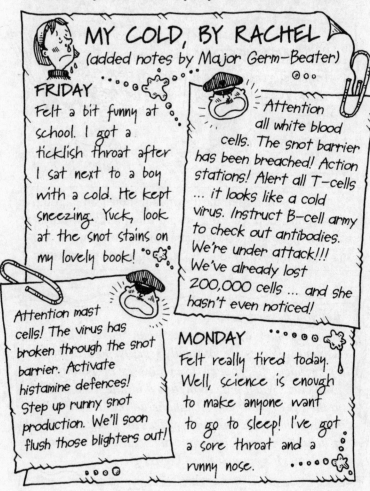

MY COLD, BY RACHEL
(added notes by Major Germ-Beater)

FRIDAY
Felt a bit funny at school. I got a ticklish throat after I sat next to a boy with a cold. He kept sneezing. Yuck, look at the snot stains on my lovely book!

Attention all white blood cells. The snot barrier has been breached! Action stations! Alert all T-cells … it looks like a cold virus. Instruct B-cell army to check out antibodies. We're under attack!!! We've already lost 200,000 cells … and she hasn't even noticed!

Attention mast cells! The virus has broken through the snot barrier. Activate histamine defences! Step up runny snot production. We'll soon flush those blighters out!

MONDAY
Felt really tired today. Well, science is enough to make anyone want to go to sleep! I've got a sore throat and a runny nose.

TUESDAY

I woke up today with a sore nose. It felt all bunged up. Had to go to school — worst luck. Felt chronic!

Histamine defences working well. White blood cells to the affected nose region.

WEDNESDAY

Terrible runny nose, I feel light-headed. Mum says I've got a fever. No school today.

Runny nasal discharge has germs on the run! But, oh dear — she's wiping her nose with used hankies and stuffing viruses back up her nostrils! Fever defence working well.

THURSDAY

I just feel like going to sleep. I'm so tired.

"Sleep" she says! Pah! We in the immune system NEVER sleep. We've been fighting non-stop for days. Phew!

FRIDAY

I'm tired and washed out.

Not half as much as us! We've lost millions of dead white blood cells ... but, we've won — well done chaps!!

SATURDAY

I'm feeling better! Just in time for the weekend!

All thanks to us!

Once you've had a disease caused by a virus or bacterium the general rule is that you shouldn't get it again. A scientist would say you're immune to that illness. (Yes, I know you get colds all the time but that's because each cold is caused by a slightly different virus.)

Deadly disease fact file

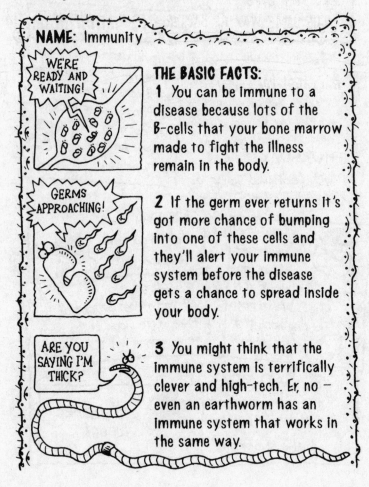

NAME: Immunity

WE'RE READY AND WAITING!

GERMS APPROACHING!

ARE YOU SAYING I'M THICK?

THE BASIC FACTS:

1 You can be immune to a disease because lots of the B-cells that your bone marrow made to fight the illness remain in the body.

2 If the germ ever returns it's got more chance of bumping into one of these cells and they'll alert your immune system before the disease gets a chance to spread inside your body.

3 You might think that the immune system is terrifically clever and high-tech. Er, no – even an earthworm has an immune system that works in the same way.

DEADLY DETAILS: If lots of people in an area are immune to a disease it can't spread widely, but if most people aren't immune then it will become a huge tidal wave of illness – an epidemic.

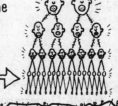

INFECTED PEOPLE MULTIPLY IN THE SAME WAY AS BACTERIA

Bet you never knew!
When an epidemic struck the cities of ancient Turkey an ugly person was chosen to be sacrificed to the gods. They ate a barley loaf, dried figs and cheese, and they were beaten with fig branches. Afterwards, the chosen person was burnt alive and their ashes scattered in the sea. Oddly enough, this practice didn't stop the epidemic and no, your teacher wouldn't have been the victim so stop daydreaming and read on…

So why aren't there epidemics everywhere? Come to think of it why aren't we all *dead*? Well, a few hundred years ago, as you'll discover later, there *were* massive outbreaks of disease but today many diseases are under control – thanks to the work of the people in the next chapter. Who are these wonderful people? Well, some people call them "miracle workers". Let's go meet them.

ANXIOUS ANTIGEN

GULP!

MEDICAL MIRACLES

In a world full of deadly diseases you can rely on two friends.

1 YOUR IMMUNE SYSTEM   **2** YOUR DOCTOR

Though if your doctor's Dr Grimgrave you'll have to make do with your immune system. Anyway, talking about medics, it's time to meet the people who dedicate their lives to fighting deadly diseases…

SPOT THE SCIENTIST

Let's imagine your school has been hit by a mystery ailment – the dreaded "Green Teacher Disease". Teachers and (I'm afraid) pupils, are turning green and developing smelly purple boils.

SCHOOL CLOSED DUE TO OUTBREAK OF GREEN TEACHER DISEASE!

A team of scientists is desperately trying to find a cure. Here they are…

① IMMUNOLOGIST
(im-mu-nol-lo-gist)

Studies how the immune
system fights the disease.
The immunologist is looking
at blood samples from the
sufferers to discover if
they're making antibodies
to fight the disease
antigens. An immunologist
knows the difference
between an antibody and an
antigen (check back to
page 37 if you're not
sure).

ABSENT-MINDED
LOOK.

TEST-TUBE
CONTAINING AN
INTERESTING
BLOOD SAMPLE.

② BACTERIOLOGIST/VIROLOGIST

Bacteriologists (back-teer-re-ol-lo-gists)
study bacteria and virologists (vi-rol-lo-
gists) study (that's right!) viruses – and
between them they are trying to find the
germs that cause Green
Teacher Disease. (They could
be bacteria or viruses – we
don't know yet.) Both
scientists want to search
for the germs in samples of
blood and skin and snot and diseased matter
from the purple boils. The bacteriologist
will try to spot the germs through a
microscope but since viruses are far
smaller than bacteria, the virologist will
use the more powerful electron microscope
for her work.

REMEMBER THESE?
FROM PAGES 19-24

VIRUS

BACTERIA

CONTINUED ➤

45

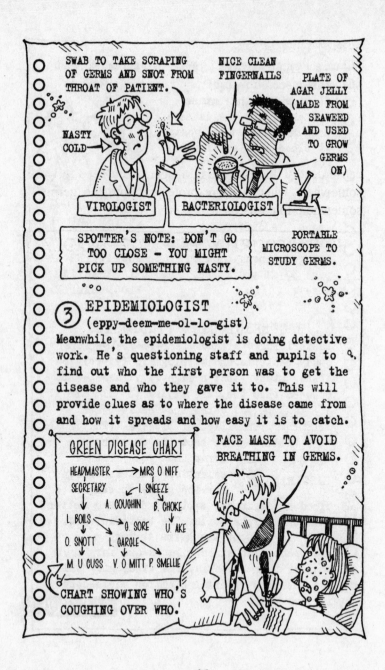

SWAB TO TAKE SCRAPING OF GERMS AND SNOT FROM THROAT OF PATIENT.

NICE CLEAN FINGERNAILS

PLATE OF AGAR JELLY (MADE FROM SEAWEED AND USED TO GROW GERMS ON)

NASTY COLD

VIROLOGIST

BACTERIOLOGIST

SPOTTER'S NOTE: DON'T GO TOO CLOSE – YOU MIGHT PICK UP SOMETHING NASTY.

PORTABLE MICROSCOPE TO STUDY GERMS.

③ EPIDEMIOLOGIST
(eppy-deem-me-ol-lo-gist)

Meanwhile the epidemiologist is doing detective work. He's questioning staff and pupils to find out who the first person was to get the disease and who they gave it to. This will provide clues as to where the disease came from and how it spreads and how easy it is to catch.

GREEN DISEASE CHART

HEADMASTER → MRS O NIFF

SECRETARY

I. SNEEZE

A. COUGHIN   B. CHOKE

L. BOILS → O. SORE   U. AKE

O. SNOTT   L. GAROLE

M. U CUSS   V. O MITT P. SMELLIE

CHART SHOWING WHO'S COUGHING OVER WHO.

FACE MASK TO AVOID BREATHING IN GERMS.

WHERE THEY WORK

All these scientists work in university laboratories and in specialist research institutes such as the Pasteur Institute in Paris or the Center for Disease Control in Atlanta, USA. Immunologists also work in hospital laboratories where they advise doctors on how well patients are resisting diseases. Scientists who work with germs that cause deadly diseases are in danger. They need to work somewhere where they're protected from the germs – somewhere like this...

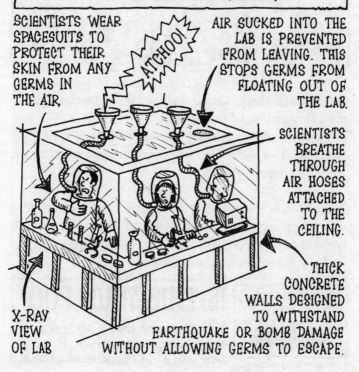

HIGH-SECURITY LAB (FOR DEADLY INCURABLE DISEASES)

SCIENTISTS WEAR SPACESUITS TO PROTECT THEIR SKIN FROM ANY GERMS IN THE AIR

ATCHOO!

AIR SUCKED INTO THE LAB IS PREVENTED FROM LEAVING. THIS STOPS GERMS FROM FLOATING OUT OF THE LAB.

SCIENTISTS BREATHE THROUGH AIR HOSES ATTACHED TO THE CEILING.

THICK CONCRETE WALLS DESIGNED TO WITHSTAND EARTHQUAKE OR BOMB DAMAGE WITHOUT ALLOWING GERMS TO ESCAPE.

X-RAY VIEW OF LAB

47

COULD YOU BE A SCIENTIST?

So how would you get on as a germ scientist?

1 Have you got the right gut instinct? In 1982 Australian scientist Barry Marshall became convinced that the painful ulcers some people get in their stomachs were caused by bacteria. It was a gut instinct all right – but certain germs always seemed to be in the victims' stomachs. Barry decided on an experiment...

What did he do?

a) He cut open a healthy patient's stomach and added the bacteria to see what would happen.

b) He tried growing the germs in a bowl of school dinner custard. The slimy custard was the closest he could get to the slimy insides of the stomach.

c) He drank the disgusting bacteria and stuck a viewing tube called an endoscope into his own stomach to check what they were up to.

2 In 1948 scientists were searching for a person who was spreading the germs that caused the deadly disease typhoid in their poo. How did they find the person?

a) They placed an advert in the paper.

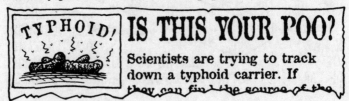

48

b) They tested everyone in town for the disease.

c) They ran tests on the sewage and found the germ and then tested all the sewage pipes, crawling through the sewers until they found the toilet that the person was using.

CAREFUL IT'S REALLY DEEP HERE

SPLOSH!

CRAWL!

DON'T WORRY, I'VE GOT A SNORKEL

CRAWL! SPLOSH!

CRAWL! SPLOSH!

Answers: 1 c) Barry found that the germs were busy making ulcers. **2 c)** It was smelly, but it worked.

HOW DID SCIENTISTS DISCOVER THAT GERMS CAUSE DISEASE?

It's a good question because germs can be quite hard to investigate. They come in a confusing number of varieties and none of them carry signs saying:

HI! WE'RE GERMS AND WE'RE HERE TO CAUSE DISEASES.

EARLY IDEAS

Some ancient doctors suspected that unseen creatures caused disease. Roman medic Marcus Terentius Varro

(116-27 BC) reckoned that disease was caused by tiny living things that were too small to see. He was right, of course, but he couldn't prove it.

But despite Varro's ideas most ancient doctors thought the gods caused disease. We've brought together two of them to argue their cases...

Four hundred years ago doctors thought that diseases were caused by revolting smells. Luckily this isn't true, otherwise your brother or sister's trainers could spark a major health alert.

Even after the microscope was invented in 1609, scientists refused to believe that tiny germs could kill a person – it was like saying ants could slay elephants.

The first clue that germs were less innocent than they seemed came in the 1860s when French scientist Louis Pasteur (1822–1895) investigated a disease that attacked silkworms (the caterpillars that spin silk). Pasteur found the disease was caused by protozoa and that a nasty bacterium caused silkworm diarrhoea. But you couldn't just collar a particular germ and say "Oi, you're nicked for causing this 'ere illness." For one thing, there are loads of germs which made pinning the blame on one of them a bit hit or miss.

A pushy doctor was to change all that…

Hall of fame: Robert Koch (1843–1910)
Nationality: German

Young Robert Koch had 13 brothers and sisters. Can you imagine how he suffered? Thirteen brothers and sisters all trying to boss you around.

Well, anyway, Robert was a clever lad and his science-minded granddad and uncle encouraged him to build up a collection of dead insects and other grisly specimens. Later, at the University of Gottingen, one of his teachers persuaded young Robert to take up medicine and he became a doctor, first in the Army and later on in Wollstein, Germany.

But he became more and more interested in germs. He turned his consulting room into a lab and in 1871, his wife gave him a microscope for his birthday.

Can you guess what he wanted it for? No, not for searching the cat's fur for fleas. He used it to take an even closer look at germs.

And so Koch came to study an especially disgusting disease called anthrax. This causes revolting sores on the lungs and can kill humans and animals.

Koch used dyes to stain some bacteria so he could see them clearly under the microscope. He next proved that it really was these bacteria that caused the diseases by injecting them into some cute little mice and making them ill. (I suppose they could have been saved by mouse to mouse resuscitation.)

COULD YOU BE A SCIENTIST?

What did Koch feed his anthrax bacteria on?

a) Chocolate

b) Wood shavings

c) The watery jelly-like stuff from the inside of an eyeball mixed up with blood.

CLUE: Think of where anthrax bacteria might like to eat.

Answer: c) At this point agar jelly hadn't been invented. The anthrax germs happily multiplied on the tasty gloop. (Of course, anthrax is a disease of animals so the germs fed on bits of animal.) By the way, Koch invented agar jelly a few years later.

Koch had proved for the first time ever that germs cause disease in humans. And he used his work to develop four postulates.

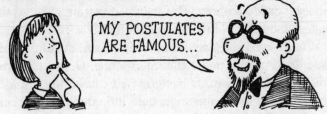

Do you say…?

Answer: A "postulate" has nothing to do with pustules. It's a posh word for a suggestion. Now my postulate is that you read on and stop asking silly questions!

Koch's suggestions were important because they outlined a new approach to studying disease. Here's Robert Koch back from the dead to explain them.

Oh – a quick warning. As a result of his discoveries he did become rather big-headed…

54

DEAD BRAINY: THE GREAT ROBERT KOCH

I, the great Robert Koch, will explain my four postulates that have changed the history of the world. I will use as my example the severe sore throat that I have developed since I've been dead. I've been dying for a cough in my coffin.

In order to prove that a germ causes disease...

Postulate 1. You must find the germ living in the body in the same place as the disease. I took a swab of my throat and discovered this bacterium.

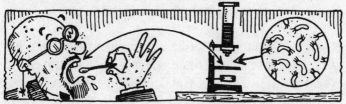

Postulate 2. You must be able to grow the germ so that it divides several times. I have succeeded in growing the germ in a plate of beef soup that has been cooked into a jelly.

Postulate 3. By giving the germs to a healthy animal you make the animal sick. I have succeeded in doing this to a rabbit.

Postulate 4. You must next find the germs living inside the animal. I have taken a sample from the rabbit and found the germs have multiplied in its throat.

This proves that although I have been dead for some time I am still a great world-famous scientist.

Koch was right. The German government gave him his very own research institute. He also got to travel the world cutting up bodies and investigating deadly but fascinating diseases. For Koch it was a dream job. His two greatest discoveries, in 1882 and 1884, were the germs that cause the deadly diseases TB and cholera. (You can find out more on pages 21 and 96.) In 1905 Koch was awarded the Nobel Prize for his work.

Between them, Koch and his rival, Frenchman Louis Pasteur, encouraged a whole new group of scientists to plunge into the world of deadly diseases and go searching for the germs that caused them. And the scientists had a powerful new weapon to fight infection: vaccines. Here's all the vital facts you need to know about those necessary jabs…

PASS YOUR SCIENCE TEST WITH HORRIBLE SCIENCE

1 What is a vaccine?

It's a sample of weakened germs. The germs can be weakened by keeping them low on food or heating them to a temperature that they find uncomfortable. Either way, the germs should find it hard to multiply – yes, a bit like some kids in a maths test, ha ha.

2 How does a vaccine work?

By injecting the germs into a person you can get their immune system (B-cells and T-cells) to recognize the germ and get ready for a bit of fisticuffs. Of course the weakened germs aren't a threat, but if the same germs get into the body the white blood cells will be ready and waiting.

ARGH! THEY'RE WAITING FOR US!

3 How were vaccines discovered?

In 1796 Edward Jenner (1749–1823) discovered how to use pus from the sores made by the milder disease, cowpox, to prevent smallpox. Although Jenner didn't understand about immunity, the virus that causes cowpox is similar to smallpox so the body can use immunity against one to fight the other. Jenner was on the right lines even if his scratch wasn't a true vaccine because he didn't use actual smallpox germs. Then, in 1879 Louis Pasteur investigated chicken cholera. (Any guesses what animal this disease infects?)

Pasteur went on holiday leaving a sample of the germs in a nice tasty broth – lucky no one ate it whilst he was away. On his return, Pasteur was amazed to find that when he injected the disease into, yes, you got it, chickens – the birds *didn't* fall ill. As Pasteur found out, the weakened germs made the chickens immune to the disease. Bet that gave him something to crow about!

PHEW! I THOUGHT WE WERE COCK-A-DOODLE-DOOMED!

NEW DRUG FACTS

The doctors soon had another weapon. Scientists were rapidly discovering that certain substances killed bacteria but not the living cells of the body that they lived amongst…

1 The first germ-killing substance was salvarsan, found by German scientist Paul Ehrlich (1854–1915) in 1909. Ehrlich had been searching for new germ-killing substances and salvarsan was effort number 606. And I thought third time was supposed be lucky, not 606th!

WHOOPEE! CAN I GO HOME, NOW?

2 Many early germ-killing drugs were actually dyes. German scientists noticed that the dyes stained and killed bacteria and left human cells untouched. One famous example was prontosil found by Gerhard Domagk in 1932 (1895–1964). Unfortunately the red dye turned the patient bright red!

I FEEL GREAT!

WELL, THERE'S NO NEED TO BE EMBARRASSED!

3 Within four years French scientists had found that the germ-killing part of the drug was actually a substance called sulphonamide (sul-fon-a-myde) that had already been discovered in 1908. So poor Domagk was left red in the face.

4 Scientists began to develop new drugs based on the sulphonamide chemicals and by 1947 they had made over 5,000 varieties!

Oddly enough though, some of the most powerful germ-killing substances are made not in test tubes but in living cells. Wonderful chemicals that rescue people from the jaws of death. Why not inject a bit of life into your day and read the next chapter?

It could prove a lifesaver...

LUCKY LIFESAVERS

Doctors have two more weapons in the battle against deadly disease: antitoxins and antibiotics. And if you thought I said "ant-tick-tock" (an insect alarm clock?) you'd better read this next bit...

AMAZING ANTITOXINS

Antitoxins are antibodies from a person or animal that has had a disease. They can be injected into another person to help them fight the disease, a process also known as "serum therapy". This breakthrough was made by two scientists working for Robert Koch, German Emil von Behring (1854–1917) and Japanese Shibasaburo Kitasato (1852–1931).

SERUM THERAPY? I DON'T GET THE POINT

YOU WILL!

COULD YOU BE A SCIENTIST?

The scientists injected toxins from a deadly kind of bacteria called tetanus into a rabbit. The rabbit hadn't received enough toxin to kill it and it made antibodies to the toxins. The scientists then injected these into mice. They then gave the toxins to the mice.

What happened?

a) The mice grew extra long ears and nibbled lettuce.

b) The mice stayed healthy.

c) The mice died.

Answer: b) The rabbit antitoxins protected the mice. In 1894 Von Behring used this technique to get a horse to make antitoxins that could be given to children to fight the deadly disease diphtheria.

A NOTE TO THE READER...

Homework can be a problem – especially when you haven't done it. Nowadays, teachers are quite sophisticated and no longer believe perfectly reasonable excuses like:

What you need is a new set of excuses – like you're suffering from a deadly disease. If you're lucky you might even get the next six weeks off school! Anyway, free with this book you get a set of sick notes. Simply copy them out and fill in your name in the spaces and post them to your teacher!

SICKENING SICK NOTE 1: DIPHTHERIA

Dear teacher,
I'm really scared about poor little me
.... I've s/he's got
disgusting, oozing throat sores and now
they've formed a horrible thick slimy
layer. It's TERRIBLE! Poor ....
can't drink soup without it dribbling
out of her/his nostrils! Her/his
condition is dreadfully desperate - s/he
can hardly breathe! The doctor says
it's diphtheria - so I hope you'll
understand that .... hasn't done
any of my homework.
Signed,

A concerned parent

Sickening sick note notes

1 With diphtheria, the bacteria make toxins that poison the nerves and stop them from working. This can lead to heart failure and death.

2 And if that doesn't happen the victim is slowly suffocated by the slimy germs. No wonder the Spanish call the disease "garrotillo" from "garrotte" – a form of strangulation.

CHOKE A LOT?

I'M SUFFOCATING AND YOU'RE OFFERING ME SWEETS?

3 But on the plus side you do get a few days off school … and maybe more!

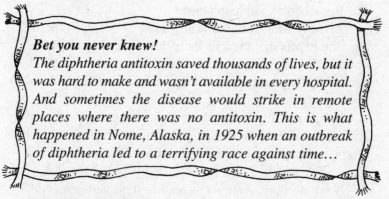

THE MIRACLE DOGS

Nome, Alaska, January 1925

Anna was dying. The nine-year-old girl had little time left but mercifully she didn't know it. Her breathing was uneasy as the diphtheria took a grip. Outside, the wind howled and snow banked up above the windows. It seemed as if the little hospital was lost in a world of ice under the dark skies of winter.

Dr Curtis Welch paced up and down the ward. The worry lines pinched his forehead and his eyes hurt because they hadn't closed for two nights. Five times the town's radio telegraph operator had called for help for the sick children in his care. All had diphtheria and they needed antitoxin desperately.

But when would help come?

Already four children were dead, slowly smothered by the germs that bred in their throats. Twenty children were sick, of whom Anna was the worst. And Dr Welch knew that without antitoxin the disease would kill them all, one by one.

He glared angrily at the swirling snow. If only the weather would ease, a supply might get through! But it kept on snowing – for hour after hour. The snow looked set to fall for ever.

Next morning, Americans read in their newspapers of the plight of the children. In churches all over the nation people offered prayers. A supply of antitoxin was sent to the railhead town of Nenana – but this was 674 miles from Nome.

Meanwhile in Nome the Board of Health committee was arguing about how to get hold of the lifesaving medicine. Planes were the answer, declared the Mayor. Some people nodded their heads but mining boss Mark Summers, disagreed.

"The planes are grounded for the winter. But my sledge dog drivers are the best. Hell – if anyone can get through they can!" he exclaimed.

"So when can we expect the antioxin?" asked Dr Welch eagerly.

"I guess nine days, but maybe more."

"Nine days – for pity's sake – those kids don't have nine days!"

Mark Summers shook his head.

"These guys do the impossible but they ain't miracle workers."

Dr Welch felt like swearing. The exhausted doctor dared not tell his nurses about the delay. One of them was Anna's mother. She could see that her daughter was burning up with fever and every so often she would creep into the kitchen and sob quietly. Yes, Anna was fighting every step. But now her body was tired, desperately weak, and the germs choked her throat until she couldn't swallow. Dr Welch knew that time was running out fast.

And outside it was still snowing…

Within days the Alaska state authorites organized a relay of dog drivers. Despite the terrible weather twenty men offered to help – passing on the medicine at agreed handover points. The best of these was Mark Summers' top driver Leonhard Seppala and it was he who travelled the furthest.

On the night of 1 February it was the turn of Gunnar Kaasen to race through the blizzard. All the tough driver could hear was the panting of his dogs and the creaking of their harness and the hiss of the sledge runners and the endless howl of the ice-laden storm.

With grim pride Gunnar noted that his 13 dogs were pulling well, especially the lead dog, Balto. Gunnar had his doubts about the strong black and white huskie – was he really lead dog material? But Balto never hestitated – he seemed to know the way even as the blizzard worsened and Gunnar could scarcely see the handlebar of his sledge.

Suddenly a blast of wind caught the sledge. It lifted and rolled sideways. The dogs yelped as they tumbled in a jumble of paws and fur and twisted harness. The precious container of antitoxin fell from the sledge into deep snow. Frantically Gunnar picked himself up and untangled the dogs. Where was the antitoxin? He dug desperately in the snow with his numb, clumsy frozen hands. Surely the medicine phials were broken? Then all this would be for nothing…

At the hospital at Nome, Anna's mother watched her daughter's face by the light of an oil lamp. The child's face was so deathly pale that she looked like a waxwork – except for a thin film of sweat. Every few seconds Anna would draw a painful breath. And once her eyes opened. She gazed at her mother and said:

"I feel terrible. I'm not dying, am I?"

And Anna's mother had kissed and hugged her daughter, saying, "Hush darling, don't talk. I'm here."

After what seemed an age, Gunnar found the precious container still in its fur wrapping. But his thoughts were wandering as if they had a life of their own. He thought of the other drivers. Some dogs had dropped dead with cold and some of the drivers had arrived at their relay stations with their faces blackened by frostbite. Gunnar felt the stinging cold chewing at his cheeks as the sledge raced onwards. His mind slid in and out of consciousness. He knew he could die out here.

Suddenly as if by some strange miracle the snow stopped falling. With cold-stiffened hands, Gunnar removed his goggles. A little distance away he could make out buildings half-buried by snow.

Where was he? Nome? No, impossible. Yes – yes, YES! They had reached Nome! The streets were deep in snowdrifts but a few early risers stood and watched in amazment. Suddenly they began to clap and cheer with delight. Slowly Gunnar made his way towards the people. But as he reached Balto he stumbled and fell, exhausted in the snow.

Soon a small crowd had gathered. They were hugging Gunnar and petting the dogs, especially Balto, who stood silent with exhaustion, too weary to wag his tail.

All the nurses were there except one who stood by Anna's bedside with tears streaming down her face.

"You're safe now," she whispered to the unconscious girl. "You're going to live."

Bet you never knew!
The newspapers hailed a miracle. In just five incredible days the drivers and their dogs had beaten the weather to deliver the precious medicine. Not a single dose of antitoxin had been lost. Today children in Central Park, New York play around a statue of Balto but the glory belongs to all the drivers, most of them native Athabaskan and Inuit, who risked their lives to save the children of Nome.

AMAZING ANTIBIOTICS

Three years later a scientist discovered an amazing substance called an antibiotic that killed bacteria (but not viruses). The substance was made into a new drug called penicillin that could literally snatch people from the jaws of death, and its discoverer won the Nobel Prize and became an international superstar. His name was Alexander Fleming (1881–1955) and he's so famous your teacher will know all about him – won't she/he?

Well, *won't* she/he? Let's find out…

OF COURSE I KNOW ALL ABOUT ALEXANDER FLIM, ER, FLOM, ER, FLAM, ER...

FLEMING!

TEST YOUR TEACHER

1 How did Fleming get his first medical job?
a) His natural genius impressed other scientists.
b) He was a crack rifle shot.
c) The other scientists needed someone to make tea.

2 During the First World War Fleming treated wounded soldiers in France. What experiment did he perform to help them?
a) He used slug juice to heal wounds.
b) He made a model wound and filled it with germs to test whether germ-killing chemicals worked properly.
c) He tried to use cold tea to kill germs.

3 What was Fleming's favourite hobby?
a) Gardening.
b) Painting pictures using germs.
c) Collecting used tea bags.

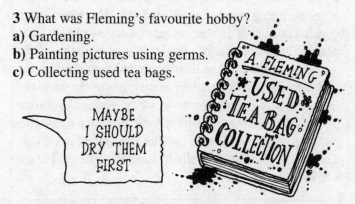

4 In 1921 Fleming discovered the germ-killing chemical in mucus. How did he make this breakthrough?
a) A dollop of snot fell from his nose on to a sample of germs.
b) He made the substance by mixing chemicals in a test tube.
c) He found that tea leaves didn't rot when they were wrapped in a snotty handkerchief.

Answers: 1 b) No, Fleming DIDN'T shoot his boss at the job interview! The hospital where Fleming was a student had a prize-winning rifle team. Fleming was a member of the team and his bosses were keen for him to stay.

2 b) Fleming melted some glass into the shape of a revolting deep jagged wound. He found that germs could lurk in the corners of the wound where germ-killing chemicals couldn't reach them. This encouraged Fleming to treat wounds by washing them and bandaging them rather than using the chemicals.

3 b) Fleming painted pictures using germs. Different germs have different colours and Fleming drew the pictures in agar jelly with needles dipped in the germs. The germs grew on the jelly to form the picture. Fancy one on your wall?

4 a) One day Fleming had a cold and snot from his runny nose fell on some germs and killed them.

(Unfortunately the germ-killing chemical, lysozyme, wasn't powerful enough to make into a drug but Fleming became interested in natural germ-killers.)

What your teacher's score means
0–1 Lucky the school inspectors didn't hear about this.

2–3 Fair, but remind your teacher that a higher score will be required the next time you test them.
4 Too good to be true.
Note all the **c)** answers seem to be about tea and if your teacher kept saying "**c)**" it's probably because she's longing for a tea-break. This attitude is not acceptable in one who is supposed to be educating the young.

A MOULDY OLD STORY

It's a fact that raw penicillin is made by a rare type of mould that Fleming found growing on one of his agar plates. The story has often been told but here's a *Horrible Science* exclusive – the mould gets to tell its *own* story!

MY STORY
BY PENNY CILLIUM

Surprised you want to talk to me. Me being an 'umble mould and all that. In all these years no one's ever asked for my side of the story, even though it was me and me mouldy friends what made this stuff millions of years before humans got their hands on it. Well, anyway 'ere's what *really* happened.

I first saw the light of day in St Mary's hospital, back in 1928. A scientist was researching moulds and I started my life as a little spore what blew upstairs and landed on a plate of jelly in Fleming's lab. *Strawberry or lime?* I asked meself. Sorry, just a mouldy joke. The jelly was boiled seaweed. But I'm not fussy – if it's food, it's food.

Fleming was growing bacteria from an infected boil on the plate – but I soon put a stop to that. Well, I mean, I know I'm only 'umble but would *you* want someone oozing boils over your dinner? So I squirted some germ-killing stuff we moulds make and that kept the germs away. Success on a plate, I thought.

So where was Fleming whilst I was hard at

72

work? Well, I'm only an 'umble mould and no one tells me nothing but I found out later he was on holiday. Scotland to be exact – very nice! And get this ...

when he comes back he only dumps me in a bucket of disinfectant! Lucky, I was on top of the pile of other plates otherwise no one would have heard of penicillin!

Wasn't till a pal of his dropped by and spotted me that Fleming got interested. That's when the trouble started – he started doing tests and one of his mates nibbled me to see if I was poisonous! Wish I had been!!! In the end Fleming used me juice to kill unwanted germs on his precious germ dishes. And that was me life for years – cleaning up for a lazy scientist! I'm only 'umble, but well, would you want to spend yer life washing dishes?

Years later humans learnt how to make my juice stronger using chemicals and people started saying what a hero lazy old Fleming was for finding me! Fleming and his mates got a Nobel Prize and a slap-up dinner – but did I get invited? I'm only 'umble – I'd have been happy to eat the mouldy old food scraps no one wanted! After all, that's a feast for me! But I was left stuck on that jelly dish and then can yer believe it? – I got shoved in a *museum*. Well honestly – there's gratitude for yer!

SO WHAT HAPPENED NEXT?

After Fleming spotted the mould and realized it could kill germs he got excited. The problem, as we've seen, was that Fleming's mould juice wasn't strong enough to kill germs in the body. Fleming tried investigating bits of mouldy old cheese and old books and creaky old boots and household dirt, looking for more moulds with germ-killing powers. But he never found any.

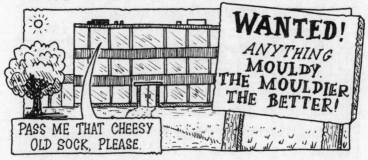

WANTED! ANYTHING MOULDY. THE MOULDIER THE BETTER!

PASS ME THAT CHEESY OLD SOCK, PLEASE.

Penicillin only saw the light of day because German-born scientist Ernst Chain (1906–1979) was looking for a germ-killing substance and read an article Fleming had written about his discovery. Chain found a way to concentrate the mould juice and make it more powerful by treating it with chemicals. Now the mould juice could really prove its worth. A little girl at St. Mary's Hospital was dying from a diseased bone marrow but huge doses of penicillin cured her in just one amazing night. By morning she was sitting up in bed feeling much better!

YESTERDAY I WAS DYING AND TODAY I'M DYING... TO GO HOME!

Chain and his Australian boss Howard Florey (1898–1968) took their idea to America, looking for help to produce penicillin on a massive scale. They found backers in a government lab in Peoria, Illinois, where scientists grew the mould on waste from corn-processing. Then local fungi expert "Mouldy" Mary Hunt found another mould growing on a melon in a local market.

It turned out that this mould, a relative of the one that Fleming had found, was even better at making germ-killing juice! And for ten years, until scientists learnt how to make the drug in a test tube, this mould supplied the world with penicillin.

AMAZING MOULD FACTS

1 Yep – there's no doubt about it, moulds are good for you. Well, some are. In the Ukraine and parts of England mouldy slices of bread were used as traditional bandages. And yes, the mould stopped germs from infecting the wounds.

2 You might never have been treated with penicillin but if you've ever eaten Stilton cheese you've *eaten* it. That's because a mould related to the one that makes the drug gives stilton its delicious pongy flavour.

THE SMELL WILL MAKE YOU SICK, BUT THE MOULD WILL MAKE YOU BETTER

REVOLTING STINK!

3 Scientists have since found more mouldy antibiotics. One type are the cephalosporins (cef-fal-lo-spoor-rins) made by a kind of fungus. They were found by scientist Giuseppe Brotzu (1895–1976) by a seaside sewage pipe. The fungi were greedily scoffing the rotting poo. But NO, paddling in sewage doesn't always guarantee a great scientific discovery so don't try it.

4 Another antibiotic was discovered by a team of boffins led by American scientist Selman Waksman (1888–1973). Glory-hunting Selman was so keen he tested over 10,000 (yes, you did read that right, TEN THOUSAND) suitable microbes. But it was actually his student Albert Schatz who found the promising bacteria … in the throat of a chicken.

WHOOPEE! GROAN!

So would you volunteer to poke around in a chicken's gullet? Or would you turn chicken? In the end Waksman was the winner. He was awarded the Nobel Prize in 1952 – which was a bit odd because he hadn't been around when Schatz made his dramatic diccovery. It sounds a bit like fowl play to me!

DEADLY EXPRESSIONS

A scientist says…

IT'S STREPTOMYCES (STREP-TOE-MY-SEES)

Do you say…?

IT'S STEPPED IN YOUR WHAT?

Answer: No. It's the name of the microbe Waksman found.

Streptomyces proved good for bumping off the bacteria that cause TB and other deadly diseases such as plague. These horrific germs make the other microbes you've seen so far seem warm and caring!

Wanna know more? I hope so cos THEY'RE LURKING IN THE NEXT CHAPTER

RAGING PLAGUE

This is a story about a human, a rat, a flea and a bacterium. It tells how the bacterium made everyone's lives (and deaths) a complete misery and how between them they killed hundreds of millions of people and caused hundreds of years of misery. Would you fancy a dose of plague? Why not read on – it's the most painless way to find out!

SICKENING SICK NOTES 2: THE PLAGUE (AKA THE BLACK DEATH)

Dear teacher,

TERRIBLE NEWS! My poor little .... had the Black Death last night so s/he didn't do ~~my~~ any homework. It all began with an agonizing headache and fever and then ~~my~~ her/his lymph nodes filled with germs and pus and swelled to the size of apples! S/he was in AGONY! Horrible lumps of bacteria formed under her/his skin causing black blotches - I don't know what to do! He/she might die and then ~~I~~ he/she might not go to school for ages!

Signed,

~~Me~~ A con very concerned parent.

Sickening sick note notes
(Don't forget to read this bit!)

1 Plague is caused by a bacterium called *Yersina pestis*. But this tiny pest is far from tiny in its effects. If the disease isn't treated with antibiotics at least one third of its victims *die* in five days.

2 Sometimes plague attacks the brain and blood and sometimes it dissolves the lungs. The victims cough germs everywhere and spread the disease.

3 Whatever happens, death is usually caused by the toxins that the germs make and huge lumps of germs breaking up vital bits of the body.

Sounds like fun, I DON'T think. But how does this horrible disease spread? Well, let's imagine a rat, a flea, a human and the bacterium all kept diaries… (OK – this *is* going to take quite a leap of imagination, or in the flea's case quite a hop.)

DEADLY DIARIES

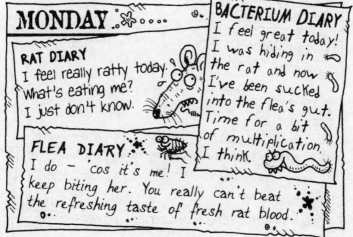

MONDAY

RAT DIARY
I feel really ratty today. What's eating me? I just don't know.

BACTERIUM DIARY
I feel great today! I was hiding in the rat and now I've been sucked into the flea's gut. Time for a bit of multiplication, I think.

FLEA DIARY
I do – 'cos it's me! I keep biting her. You really can't beat the refreshing taste of fresh rat blood.

BACTERIUM DIARY
So you should – you've got thousands of us in every drop of your blood. Hey gang – let's go and check out the old lungs.

FRIDAY

HUMAN DIARY I've got stinking breath and I'm coughing up blood.

BACTERIUM DIARY
Hmm, don't reckon this one will last much longer. It's about time we found another victim ... anyone fancy a nice juicy rat?

Bet you never knew!
1 Rats actually find the plague more deadly than humans but who cares about them? Actually, I've heard some teachers have pet rats and cuddle these vicious rodents and call them soppy names like Tufty – but it's hard to imagine.
2 Although the main way the flea passes on the bacteria to humans is through bites, other methods include…
a) Rubbing flea poo into the open wound made by the bite. (Flea poo always *contains bacteria.)*
b) Crunching a flea in your mouth. The flea blood is full of bacteria and if it gets on your tonsils the bacteria can sometimes ooze into your blood. Lovely!

So that's how the bacteria can get into your body. But where did the plague come from? Who got it first – the rats, the fleas or the humans? Well, the loathsome life story of the plague is about to be revealed...

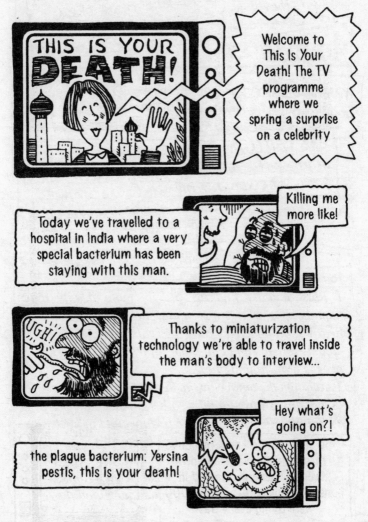

Your early life was rather obscure wasn't it? It's thought that you lived in Central Asia.

Well, yes it was over 100,000 years ago but my memory's a bit hazy now. I do remember being happy living amongst the wild marmots in their warm burrows.

They never got a nasty disease?

No, I got on well with them. Well, all right, their immune systems stopped me multiplying but they couldn't wipe me out.

Then you teamed up with your long-suffering partners the black rat and its fleas. Together you travelled the world living in ships and houses.

Er yes, but we've never got on very well.

And here they are...

Grrr — you make us sick — we're going to get you!

Er hi guys!

Yeah — it was a busy time.

You soon got to know millions of people all over Asia and Europe. When you arrived in Constantinople in AD 542, 10,000 were dying every day.

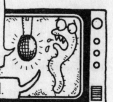

THE PUTRID PLAGUE

Every few years the plague struck cities all over Europe killing old and young, rich and poor. And wherever the plague went it spread sorrow, misery and death. Often people fled their homes to get away from the disease and families split up.

Of course the authorities did all they could do to fight the menace (which wasn't a lot). Which of these anti-plague rules are genuine?

PLAGUE RULES OK?

Answer TRUE or FALSE.

To fight ye plague...

1 All ye cats and dogs must be killed (and that goes for ye – Tiddles).

2 Everyone coming from plague-stricken areas must spend up to 40 days in isolation from the rest of ye town.

3 Everyone who hath the plague is to be made to take a nice hot bath twice a day on pain of ye death.

4 Paint a red cross on ye door and order ye entire family to stay at home. Leave food and medicine on ye doorstep and send ye old women to check if they be dead yet.

5 If anyone sneaks out they will be executed in front of their own house.

6 Anyone with ye plague is to be given £100 on condition that they leave town at once.

7 If ye fall sick of ye plague ye house will be burnt down and all ye belongings burnt.

Answers: 1 True. In London in 1665 plague killed 75,000 people and all the cats and dogs were killed to stop the plague spreading. In fact, cats and dogs do actually suffer from the disease but killing them did little good because, of course, the fleas carried on biting humans and spreading the disease.

2 True. This precaution was developed in Ragusa (now in Croatia) in 1377. It became known as quarantine and when it was properly enforced it stopped the plague from spreading.

3 False. In 1348 doctors at the University of Paris warned that bathing opened up pores in the skin and would let diseases into the body. This was "pore" advice. But nowadays children are still forced to take a bath on pain of death.

4 True. This is what happened in London in 1665. Unfortunately when we say "old women" we're not talking sweet white-haired old dears – we're talking killer grannies. The old women often robbed the dead and strangled those who weren't quite dead enough. In 1348 gravediggers committed this grisly crime in Florence, Italy.

5 True. This was a rule from Scotland. In 1530 a tailor was hanged in front of his house for going to church when his wife was ill. Luckily the rope broke so the man was kicked out of town instead.

6 False.

7 True. Queen Elizabeth of England (1533–1603) ordered the belongings of sick people to be burned – this was sensible because the fire killed the fleas. The same is true for burning houses, a measure used in Hawaii in 1899. Unfortunately the fire lit in one house got out of control and destroyed 5,000 more. I expect the person responsible got a warm reception.

Bet you never knew!
In the English village of Eyam in 1665 a bundle of cloth sent from the plague-stricken city of London brought fleas and the plague. Within four days the man who had received the cloth was dead. Bravely, the villagers decided to quarantine their village, letting no one in or out so that the plague wouldn't spread. Then one by one, they died. By the following spring, of the 350 villagers, just 84 were left alive. But thanks to their bravery the plague spread no further.

Of course, the true causes of plague hadn't been discovered yet. But doctors tried every cure you can think of and a few that you'd never think of in a thousand years. Needless to say they were as useless as an odour-free stink bomb.

☠ HORRIBLE HEALTH WARNING!

Did you hear me? I said they were U–S–E–L–E–S–S. So don't even *think* of trying any of these cures on yourself or your little brother/sister/pet plague rat. Some of these "cures" were DANGEROUS!

87

Chapter Two
A BREATH OF FRESH AIR

As everyone knows, ye plague be caused by some kind of nasty smell in ye air. So it helps if you...

Light ye bonfires or set off ye cannon. Smoke gets rid of ye smell. Smoking tobacco is _good_ for ye because it gets rid of smells. Everyone should smoke including ye children.

HISTORICAL NOTE: Cannons and tobacco were seventeenth century, the others were 1348. Children were beaten by their teacher at Eton College, England, for _not_ smoking.

WHACK!

BUT SMOKING IS **BAD** FOR YOU!

DING! DONG!

To get ye air moving in a healthy way try letting birds fly round ye room or ringing a few bells. If ye don't have ye gunpowder or ye birds or ye bells ye needs to fart into ye bottle and uncork it to let out ye odour. Ye whiff will chase out ye foul air that causeth plague (and ye friends too). If ye have not ye bottle why not simply stick ye head down ye blocked toilet?

YE FARTY PONG!

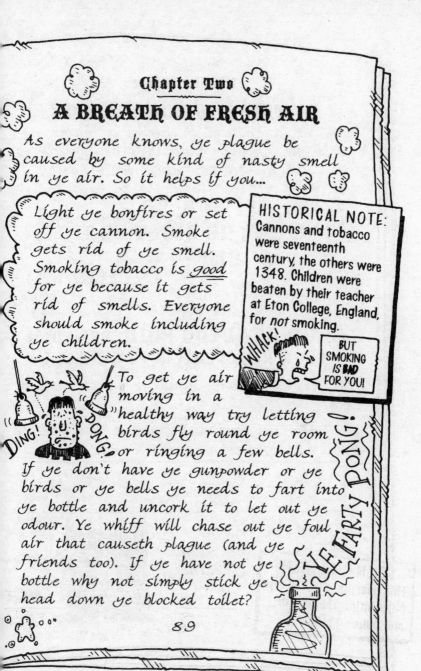

Chapter Three

BATHING IS GOOD FOR YE

No, we do not mean baths in <u>water</u> – everyone knoweth that they be <u>terribly</u> bad for ye. No, ye modern 1348 way to ward off ye plague is to bath in...

a) Vinegar

b) Your own pee (if any be left over ye can drink it twice a day)

c) Goat's pee

Chapter Four

GOOD HEALTHY SKIN: REMEDIES FROM YE SEVENTEENTH CENTURY.

If ye hath the plague ye must take care of ye skin, so...

1 Take one toad and crush it and smear ye slimy juices all over ye plague sores.

2 Rub the rump of a dead chicken on ye plague sores.

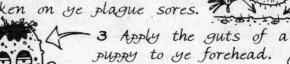

3 Apply the guts of a puppy to ye forehead.

Chapter Five
MARVELLOUS MEDICINES

Now it be time for ye medicine. That'll cure ye plague in the twinkling of an eyeball! Well, maybe.

1 Eat some crunchy dry scabs from ye plague victim's sores. They be delicious washed down with a bowl of fresh pus. (Fourteenth century)

Scabs

pus

2 Fancy something with a bit more bite? Here be a traditional seventeenth-century recipe...

a) Take the brains of a young man that hath died violently.

b) Mash well and add some wine.

c) Add a generous dollop of ye horse dung and leave to rot for a year.

NOT TO BE TAKEN BEFORE 1666

That'll doeth ye trick!

SCIENCE CLOSES IN ON THE PLAGUE GERMS

In 1855 plague was on the move again. It hit the Chinese province of Yunnan and over the next 40 years killed 100,000 people. When at last it reached the coast of China it attacked ports such as Hong Kong, and ships took the rats, the fleas, the bacteria and the plague all over the world.

Between 1896 and 1917, in India alone, over *ten million* people died. Something had to be done!

By now scientists understood that germs cause disease and thanks to Koch they knew how to perform tests to discover which germ caused a particular disease. Or so they reckoned…

In 1894 a team of scientists from Robert Koch's Institute went to Hong Kong to find the plague germ. They were led by renowned scientist Shibasaburo Kitasato (remember him from page 60). But there was another scientist in the field, Swiss-born Alexandre Yersin (1863–1943) who had worked for Louis Pasteur and had since been travelling and making maps in Vietnam. But who would make the key breakthrough?

Here's how Yersin might have recorded the next few days…

YERSIN'S DIARY 1894

SATURDAY ~ Got to Hong Kong today. Phew, it's hot - had to carry all my own bags to the humble boarding house where I'm staying. Kitasato and his 30 assistants have taken over a posh hotel in the centre of town. Well, he's welcome to it. Huh, who needs a posh place ... haven't got any nice clothes to wear anyway.

MONDAY ~ Went to the local hospital today looking for a plague victim to study and got kicked out! Seems everyone reckons that Kitasato is going to find the germ. Then the man himself turns up in his smart white suit and looks at me as if I'm something the cat brought in. OK, my armpits were a bit sweaty and I guess I could have done with a shave this morning. "You're too late, Yersin!" he sneers with a smug smile. "I've already found the germ. It was simple, I grew it from the finger of a dead plague victim!"

WEDNESDAY ~ Everyone thinks Kitasato has found the germ - but I'm not so sure. I mean, whoever heard of anyone getting plague in their finger? Lungs maybe, or lymph nodes but a finger? Anyway there's a gang of English sailors burying the dead bodies and I'm bribing them to let me cut out the rotting swollen lymph nodes from the bodies. It's smelly work, but hey ... I'm a scientist, I'm used to it. S'cuse me while I throw up!

FRIDAY ~ I've found it!!! The lymph nodes are full of fat little germs! Now all I have to do is grow them. But am I on the right track or am I wasting my time? Maybe Kitasato was right after all!

SATURDAY ~ Today I injected my germs into a healthy rat. Lucky my landlord, Yu Pai-now, doesn't know there's a rat in my room. Now all I can do is wait. Will the rat get the plague?

WEDNESDAY ~ The rat's still healthy ... oh rats! Not even a sniffle!

THURSDAY ~ No, wait, the rat's got swollen glands. He's acting as if he's drunk – he's got the plague! He's very ill. Oh yes, yes, YES – I'm so very happy!

Yersin had found the germ that causes plague and that's how it came to be named *Yersina pestis*, in his honour. Back in France he was able to make an antitoxin to the germ's toxins and two years later he was back in Hong Kong to try it out. For the first time in history people were actually cured of the plague! Today, although the plague is still around – wild animals in Asia and parts of the United States carry the disease – it can be beaten by drugs and antibiotics. The plague is still feared but it's no longer a mass killer.

Mind you, if the plague seems a pain in the guts wait till you read the next chapter…

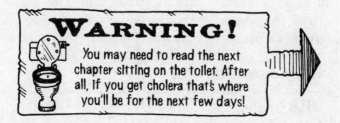

WARNING!

You may need to read the next chapter sitting on the toilet. After all, if you get cholera that's where you'll be for the next few days!

CRUEL CHOLERA

Fancy a bite to eat? Well, you'd better enjoy it now because as you read this chapter you may find your appetite disappearing. And it'll be all down to the vicious little bug that causes cholera.

WHAT'S IN A NAME?

Here's a Greek word that your teacher doesn't know: "kholera" means diarrhoea in Greek. So next time you have a bad case of the trots tell your teacher you've got a dose of cholera and you might get six months off school! But calling cholera "diarrhoea" is like calling the *Titanic* a "boat". So what would you prefer – a dose of cholera or a trip on the *Titanic*? Better read this whilst you decide…

Deadly disease fact file

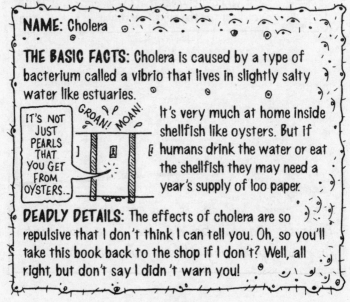

NAME: Cholera

THE BASIC FACTS: Cholera is caused by a type of bacterium called a vibrio that lives in slightly salty water like estuaries.

IT'S NOT JUST PEARLS THAT YOU GET FROM OYSTERS...

GROAN! MOAN!

It's very much at home inside shellfish like oysters. But if humans drink the water or eat the shellfish they may need a year's supply of loo paper.

DEADLY DETAILS: The effects of cholera are so repulsive that I don't think I can tell you. Oh, so you'll take this book back to the shop if I don't? Well, all right, but don't say I didn't warn you!

A DISGUSTING DIARY

Here's the journal of a Victorian lady recording the illness of her husband. Our old chum Dr Grimgrave has added his up-to-date medical comments…

Monday

1832

Oh alas! My poor Johnnie is sick. He has vomited many times and has (dare I mention this unseemly word even in the privacy of my own diary?) diarrhoea. Yet he has eaten nothing today, and prior to falling ill he had drunk but a little water. Oh woe is me! Oh woe is Johnnie!

Dr Grimgrave writes…
The stupid woman should stop blubbering and summon a doctor.

The water was crawling with cholera germs. Their toxins stop the patients bowels from doing their job of soaking up digestive juices. All these juices, containing water and minerals vital to health, are flowing out of him as diarrhoea. Without prompt treatment the patient will end up a "stiff" as we say in the medical profession.

Tuesday

Alas, poor Johnnie is worse! He is feverish and his bowels are in a constant flux and producing those unmentionable fluids. He is thirsty but sicks up anything he drinks and – horrors! – his skin has turned BLUE! And he is in agony from cramps. I called the doctor and he said he had to take blood from my beloved because he has too much! But alas – my Johnnie's blood has turned into black syrup!

Wednesday

Alas, my Johnnie is up with the angels. His skin had turned purple, then dark blue and black. And his poor dead face resembles a skull. But wait – even as I write he moves... ARGGGH! His dead body is jerking and twitching!

Dr Grimgrave writes...
That doctor should be struck off! The patient is drying out – he needs *more* liquid – not *less* blood! The drying out causes the cramps and black blood – which in turn explains the blue skin. The diarrhoea contains tiny bits of guts – hmm – I think this calls for closer examination.

Dr Grimgrave writes...
Well, the patient died as I predicted. The lack of vital body salts is resulting in signals from the dead nerves which in turn keep the dead muscles moving for a few hours. Hmm – it's a dead fascinating post-mortem phenomenon.

Sounds horrible? Sounds so horrible that you'd run a mile to get away from this disease? Well, if you don't feel like running a mile you could always take a nice relaxing holiday in some of the cholera hot-spots.

HORRIBLE SCIENCE HOLIDAYS present
A HOLIDAY WITH A DIFFERENCE
THE CHOLERA EXPERIENCE

Visit some of the most spectacular and beautiful parts of the world and spend hours and hours on the toilet (don't forget to pack the loo paper!). You'll be dying to get away!

Paris 1832
Enjoy the colour of the Paris carnival. Marvel at the revellers with their delightful painted faces and bright costumes.

CONTINUED ➤

SMALL PRINT

1. The revellers with blue faces are actually suffering from cholera but everyone thought it was just make-up until they started dying in the streets.

2. If you're not French it might be a good idea to make yourself scarce. The crowd blamed foreigners for poisoning the victims and started killing them!

3. For the REAL cholera experience why not try one of the cures suggested by Dr Francois Megendie. You lie down and he slaps 50 slimy blood-sucking leeches on your body. Note – it doesn't work, but hey, it's an experience!

FANCY A BIT OF ADVENTURE?

Try a trip to Russia in the 1890s. Experience the thrill of being a suspected cholera sufferer.

The law says that if you have cholera all your belongings are taken away and you're imprisoned in a military barracks to stop the disease spreading.

1. Life in the barracks is very harsh and you don't get much food. But at least it's cheap and cheerful.

2. If you try to escape you'll be whipped.

THINK I'LL COME BACK NEXT YEAR

YOU'LL STILL BE HERE, NEXT YEAR

No wonder a traditional Russian curse said "May you get cholera." You can try this one out on the school bully … if you dare.

COULD YOU BE A DOCTOR?

YOU are famous Victorian physician John Snow (1813–1858). You're well known for pioneering the use of the painkiller chloroform in operations and now you're interested in cholera.

In 1854 cholera breaks out in London. Thousands die, including 700 in one small corner of Soho. The people here live in slums and 54 people share an outside toilet. (How do they all fit in?)

The toilet is oozing its disgusting contents into the drinking water of the nearby pump. All the cholera victims have drunk the water. You believe that the germs that caused cholera got into the water from the toilet.

1 What do you do?

a) Take away the toilet for testing.

b) Take some water from the pump for testing.

c) Take away the pump for testing.

2 Your tests show that there are germs in the water. What do you do next?

a) Drink the water to see if you get cholera.

b) Give the water to an enemy to see if they get cholera.

c) Take the handle off the pump so no one can use it.

Answers: 1 b) When people with cholera used the toilet the germs made their way into the drinking water. The disease was slow to develop because some sufferers used potties and emptied them out of the window. It was messy if diarrhoea landed on your head but at least it kept the germs out of the water supply.

2 c) The epidemic stopped. (It was ending anyway but the important thing was that it didn't flare up again.) Snow had proved the link between cholera and dirty water.

Of course, the world sat up and took notice and Snow became a national hero! *Didn't he?* Come off it: *Horrible Science* ain't no fairy tale! No one took any notice and when John Snow died aged 44, his discovery was forgotten. Forgotten, that is, until super-doc Robert Koch took an interest in cholera.

KOCH-YA!

In 1883 cholera struck the Egyptian city of Alexandria but by the time Koch reached Egypt the cholera had all but disappeared. I bet he was gutted! Never one to miss out on research, he tried giving germs to crocodiles to see if they got cholera. If they had, they'd have shed crocodile tears!

Meanwhile Louis Pasteur had sent two assistants, Emile Roux and Louis Thuillier, to Alexandria to find the cholera germ. Unfortunately, they tried to grow germs in a broth rather than on a plate of jelly and this made it hard to sort out the many different types of germs in the broth. The two scientists became confused but Thellier still managed to catch cholera and die. Science can be tough sometimes.

Koch went to East Africa and then to Calcutta, India, in search of cholera. In Calcutta he found thousands of people suffering from the disease. Naturally, he was delighted.

He cut open ten dead bodies and tested their festering diarrhoea and vomit and local water. He found vibrio germs in all of them, proving beyond doubt that the bacteria caused cholera.

Scientific note:
Actually, Italian scientist Fillipo Pacini described finding the cholera germ in the guts of victims as early as 1854 – but no one realized that the germ actually caused the disease and Pacini's discovery was forgotten.

WARNING! REALLY REVOLTING FACTS AHEAD.

TWO REALLY REVOLTING CHOLERA STORIES

1 Even after Koch's discovery there were some who refused to believe that the disease was caused by a germ. German scientist Max von Pettenkofer (1818–1901) thought that the disease was caused by chemicals. To prove his theory he actually *drank* a revolting mixture of germs taken from the diarrhoea of a cholera victim. Von Pettenkofer got mild diarrhoea which he claimed was nothing to do with the cholera. Yeah, right.

NOT BAD, PERHAPS A LITTLE MORE PEPPER

2 Actually this experience was not unique. A nurse told John Snow how one night she was tired after a long day nursing cholera patients and she felt like a drink. She was exhausted and dazed and picked up a large cup of tea and gulped it down. Only then did she realize that it wasn't a cup of tea she was drinking … it was a potty full of diarrhoea! Amazingly, the nurse survived.

But hold on – why didn't Max and the nurse get cholera? Well, they were being protected by their stomachs. Yes, the human stomach makes a strong acid that dissolves most of the cholera germs. Wanna know more?

Dare you discover 1 … how stomach acid protects guts?

You will need:
Three glasses or jars
Yeast (the dried variety is fine)
Vinegar
Baking powder
Sugar
Three teaspoons

What you do:
1 Label the three glasses A, B and C.
2 Fill each with warm water and add three tablespoonfuls

of vinegar to B and C. Then add a heaped teaspoonful of baking powder to C and stir well until most of the froth has gone.

3 Add a teaspoonful of yeast and a heaped teaspoonful of sugar to each jar. Stir well.
4 Place the glasses in a warm place for an hour.

What do you notice?
a) Each glass contains milky beige-coloured liquid, and if I put my ear to the glasses I can hear a fizzing noise.

b) A and C are like this but not B.
c) Only B is like this, A and C are a disgusting shade of green.

Dare you discover 2 ... how to make cholera cures?

If you get cholera you're going be very interested in finding a cure. Here are two possibilities...

Cure A

You will need:

A tea bag
Some mustard
A mug
A teaspoon

What you do:

1 Fill the mug with boiling water. (Grab an adult and ask them to help.)

2 Dunk the tea bag quickly in the water.

3 Add a level teaspoon of mustard and stir well.

4 Allow five minutes to cool and try a sip. (OK, you can sniff it instead!)

Note: if you don't like it you could always add milk and give it to the adult saying:

Cure B

What you need:

A mug
Some sugar
Some salt

What you do:

1 Fill the mug with boiling water. (Apologize to adult for the horrible trick you played and ask for help.)

2 Add a heaped teaspoonful of sugar and a quarter of a level teaspoon of salt and stir well.

3 Allow five minutes to cool, and then taste.

Which cure do you think works best?

a) A

b) B

c) They're equally useful but work in different ways.

> **Answer: b)** Cure **A** is a traditional Spanish remedy and, like many old remedies, it's useless. Cure **B** is based on a mixture invented in Dacca, Bangladesh and Calcutta in the 1960s. It's designed to replace lost sugars and salts in the body and the boiling kills cholera germs in the water. This treatment has saved thousands of lives – it reverses the drying out so that the patient's white blood cells can kill off the cholera germs.

Today, cholera is still going strong in many parts of the world. Every so often the disease goes on a world tour, spread by ships that take polluted water into their ballast tanks (tanks of water that are used to stop the ship rolling in the sea) and released elsewhere. So although the disease can be cured, it's still a force to be reckoned with.

Mind you, if you think this sounds bad, in the next chapter you'll meet a whole new gang of disease-causers. They're a gang that cause really deadly diseases so you're sure to find them sickening.

Better put on that spacesuit...

VICIOUS VIRUSES

Your granny is wrong – small parcels don't always mean nice things. This chapter is about viruses – tiny things, far smaller even than bacteria. These tiny objects can ruin your life *for ever*. Fancy a closer look? Well, you'll *need* to look closer – a lot, lot closer.

Here they are…

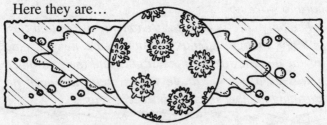

A virus is basically a chemical called DNA (or, if you want to be teacher's pet, deoxyribose nucleic acid) surrounded by another chemical called a protein. DNA, as its long name suggests, is an incredibly complicated substance.

COULD I HAVE MORE INFORMATION ON THE STRUCTURE OF DEOXYRIBOSE NUCLEIC ACID, SIR?

TEACHER'S PET

It's found in all living cells and contains millions of chemical codes that control the cell's chemistry and affect how it grows and develops. Remember that viruses hijack the cells in your body and use them to make more viruses (see pages 23–5, if you've forgotten). Well, now for the deadly details…

Deadly disease fact file

NAME: Viruses

THE BASIC FACTS ABOUT WHAT THEY DO:

1 They sneak into the body through a cut or get in through the mouth or nose.

SNEAK!

2 They land on a cell and lock on to it using their protein outer coats.

VIRUS

LAND!

CELL

3 They squeeze their DNA through the cell wall or creep in with other chemicals that are being taken into the cell.

SQUEEZE!

4 They make for the nucleus where the cell's DNA is stored and activate the DNA chemically to program the cell to make lots more viruses. (This takes about half an hour.)

Copy! Copy! Copy! Copy!

DEADLY DETAILS:

1 When the cell runs out of juice it dies and the viruses seek another victim!

SEEK! SEEK!

2 There are five million red blood cells in one drop of blood and each can hold 1,000 viruses – so there's plenty of room!

111

VICIOUS VIRUS FACTS

1 One of the body's few defences is to kill the cells that viruses infect. Unfortunately this can sometimes make things worse. The Hepatitis B virus hides inside liver cells. The immune system kills the liver cells but you need your liver to live and sometimes the body ends up killing itself! That's dead unlucky.

2 There are actually viruses called bacteriophages (back-teer-rio-fay-ges) that attack bacteria. Doesn't your heart just bleed for the little darlings?

3 When viruses copy their DNA inside a human cell they often make mistakes – known as mutations (mu-tay-shuns). Whilst some of these mistakes can harm a virus others can make it better at infecting you. For example, they make chemical changes in the outer coat that disguise the virus so that the body's defences don't spot it. Sneaky, eh? As a result, it's hard for scientists to devise vaccines for diseases caused by these viruses … diseases like flu.

FOUL FLU

Have you had flu? Sorry, silly question…

Flu is short for "influenza", which actually comes from the word "influence" and reflects an old belief that flu was caused by the influence of the stars. Well, you can thank your lucky stars if you don't get it…

Like a cold, flu is spread by coughing or sneezing droplets of spit – oh, so you knew all about that? Well, did you know that you can even spread colds and flu by *talking*?

Dare you discover ... how speaking spreads flu?

You will need:
Yourself
A good supply of spit (drink a glass of water first)
A mirror

What you do:
1 Press your nose against the mirror.
2 Say the word "SPIT" loudly.
3 Say "DRY" loudly.

113

Which letters leave the most spit on the mirror?
a) "SPIT"
b) "DRY"
c) Neither, I never spit when I talk!

Answer: a) The movement of your tongue as you speak letters such as the "P" and "T" in "SPIT" actually sprays spit. Of course, the drops of spit could be hiding millions of flu viruses. Maybe you could share this interesting information with a teacher who sprays spit as they talk. Or maybe not...

TEACHER'S TEA-BREAK TEASER

Feeling cruel? Oh good. Well, wait until your teacher gets the flu and when she drags herself into school (most teachers seem to think it's a shame if you get sent home because there's no one to teach you) hammer on the staffroom door. Smile sweetly at your suffering school teacher and ask...

Answer: Yes, it is. Everyone gets it including very old people and although it only kills about one in a thousand, with so many ill, that adds up to quite a lot of deaths. That's why flu is the biggest-killing infectious disease in the USA. But in 1918 it was worse, far worse…

THE DAILY GLOBE

31 December 1918

FATAL FLU FEAR!

This year everyone has been talking about the world-wide flu epidemic. In the USA it's said that 500,000 have died, in the UK 200,000 and in India perhaps 20 million. It's even worse than the Black Death!

Dead bodies

THE FLU CAN KILL IN 48 HOURS! In India trains have been reported full of dead passengers and in some cities the streets are full of dead bodies. Here in America many cities have banned meetings in a bid to stop the disease spreading. Cinemas have shut down and churches are closed (except for funerals).

Bodies are buried standing up to save space.

PUBLIC HEALTH ADVERT

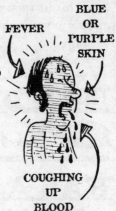

- Have you got the flu?
- Do YOU have a fever, headache, cough, has your skin turned blue or purple, are you coughing up blood? Looks like you've got the flu. Well, that's tough.
- *Don't* go out ... please!
- And *definitely* don't go near us!
- *Do* phone a funeral director – they're getting rather booked up just now.

FEVER

BLUE OR PURPLE SKIN

COUGHING UP BLOOD

Doctors' advice

We asked 20 different doctors for advice and received 21 different suggestions including ... drink coffee, take painkillers, drink alcohol, drink small doses of poison such as arsenic, eat potatoes, breathe wood-smoke, and pull your teeth and tonsils out (that'll help clear your throat).

☠ HORRIBLE HEALTH WARNING!

All these remedies were tried and they were all USELESS, so next time your little brother/sister gets flu, DON'T pull their teeth out or anything. Otherwise you'll end up in an unhealthy situation.

Bet you never knew!

1 The flu has been so deadly because it weakens the victims so much that bacteria can attack their lungs and cause the disease known as pneumonia. This results in fever, and difficulty breathing as the lungs fill with pus. Pneumonia can kill but nowadays it can be cured with antibiotics.

2 In the 1950s, American scientist Johan Hultin decided to find some of the 1918 virus. He went to a town in Alaska where the bodies of flu victims had been buried deep in the frozen ground. He dug up several preserved bodies and removed their lungs and tried to infect a ferret with the virus.

GLAD WE WEREN'T AROUND IN 1918 WITH THAT NASTY VIRUS

Unfortunately, it turned out to be dead. (That's the virus not the ferret – the ferret was no doubt relieved.)

3 After his retirement, Hultin returned to the village and dug up some more bodies. This time a team of US scientists led by Jeffrey Taubenberger studied the DNA of the virus and concluded that it came from pigs and then spread to people. It sounds a really horrible way to make a pig of yourself.

TEACHER'S TEA-BREAK TEASER

Still feeling cruel? Yippee, cos today, having shaken off her flu, your teacher's gone down with a cold! That's tragic! Once again she's dragged herself off her sick bed to come and teach you lot. Hammer boldly on the staffroom door. Your teacher will appear, clutching a dripping hankie. Smile sweetly and ask:

DID YOU CATCH YOUR COLD FROM A HORSE?

NOT YOU AGAIN!

STA

Answer: Originally, perhaps – and that's neigh kidding! Scientists have discovered that one type of cold virus is similar to a virus that affects horses. They believe that humans caught the disease thousands of years ago from their trusty steeds. Perhaps that's why your teacher's a little hoarse?

A VERY SMALL DISCOVERY

You might be wondering how scientists managed to discover viruses when they're so tiny. Well, the answer is that scientists didn't see viruses until 1930 when the electron microscope was invented. This brilliant bit of kit uses a beam of tiny blips of energy called electrons to show up tiny objects such as viruses. Sometimes it pays to think small! Before then scientists like Louis Pasteur realized that there was something causing viral diseases and they knew that it was very small because it went through the finest filters.

There was one particular virus called rabies that Pasteur struggled to make a vaccine for. It was a battle that was to have a dramatic and shocking conclusion...

Deadly disease fact file

NAME: Rabies

THE BASIC FACTS: Rabies is a virus that attacks animals such as dogs, foxes, bats, squirrels ... and humans. The disease drives the animals crazy – the dogs become mad, the bats go batty and the squirrels turn a bit nutty.

WOOF GRRR! FLAP GRRR! SQUEAK GRRR!

DEADLY DETAILS:

1 The virus heads for the brain where it blocks the nerve signals that cause swallowing. Swallowing becomes incredibly painful. Spit full of viruses dribbles out of the mouth.

2 Other symptoms are a terror of water (because the victim fears drinking because of the pain of swallowing) and violent fever.

3 Luckily, the virus is slow-moving and there's time to inject a vaccine and antibodies to defeat the virus before it reaches the brain.

A MATTER OF LIFE OR DEATH

Paris, 1937

It was late afternoon when the young American woman arrived at the gates of the Pasteur Institute. There was no one about except an old man sweeping the yard.

"Good afternoon, Mademoiselle," he said politely. "Can I help you?"

"Oh no," she said. "I merely came to see…"

"Oui," said the old man proudly. "We get many visitors like yourself, but there is no one around now." He was a thin old man with a flat cap and grey stubble on his chin.

Just then there was a rumble of thunder and it began to rain heavily.

"Oh no!" exclaimed the young woman looking crossly at the sky.

The old man shrugged. "It is impossible! I cannot work with this rain. Mademoiselle, may I offer you a cup of coffee?"

"Why yes, thank you," she smiled.

The old man led the way to a cramped room, part caretaker's shed and part storeroom of dusty laboratory supplies.

"You are interested in the great Louis Pasteur perhaps?"

"Well, I'm training to be a teacher and next semester we're doing a project on him."

The old man beamed, his eyes were misty with pleasure.

"Ah, but that is wonderful. I remember Monsieur Pasteur well."

"No kidding – you knew *the* Louis Pasteur!" said the woman in amazement.

"Oui. Perhaps you would like to hear a story about Monsieur Pasteur?"

And as he busied himself with making the coffee, the old man launched into his tale.

"It was in 1885 that Pasteur was studying the disease rabies. You are familiar with this disease?"

The young woman shuddered and nodded.

"Well, Pasteur was experimenting with a vaccine made from rabbits. Rabbits that died of rabies. Pasteur dried their backbones that were, of course, full of the virus.

He did this to weaken the virus and then he could inject it into dogs and, voilá, the dogs were protected from the rabies."

"One day a young woman knocked at his laboratory door. She had her son with her – boy named Joseph Meister who two days before had been savaged by a rabid dog."

"A *rabid dog*! Hey – that's terrible. Was the kid in a bad way?"

The old man took his time answering, carefully pouring the coffee into two chipped mugs.

"The boy had been bitten on his hands, on his legs – everywhere! He was not expected to live. Pasteur knew that he had to try the vaccine on the boy or he would die.

"I remember the scene like it was yesterday. It was evening, the blinds were drawn in the laboratory, and there was a smell of chemicals. Pasteur was there in his velvet cap, offering advice as a doctor injected the boy with vaccine. Injected! Pah – it was more like being stabbed in the belly! Of course the boy was scared, very, very scared. But he was brave and did not cry out."

The old man stirred his coffee.

"And after the injection all anyone could do was wait. Wait and wait to see whether the injection would work. Wait to see if the boy would live … or die."

There was a long silence broken only by a rumble of thunder.

"And did the boy die?" asked the woman anxiously.

"No – he did not. In fact, he is alive and well! Mademoiselle, I shall pretend no longer – the boy in the story was me. My name is Joseph Meister!" The old man's voice shook. "Louis Pasteur saved my life. That night I promised myself that I would serve Pasteur in any way I could. And I have worked here all my life – so you see, I kept my word."

His voice was stronger now and full of pride. And the face of the old man who was Joseph Meister wrinkled into a smile as he slowly sipped his coffee.

MORE VICIOUS VIRUSES

Viruses come in all shapes and sizes (though they are all fairly tiny). Here are two that you might have come across, and as usual Dr Grimgrave has all the bad news…

Dear Ms Ake,
You're suffering from the viral disease –
mumps. It's caused by a virus that
infects the spit-making glands on the
sides of your face. It gets
better on its own so go to bed
and take painkillers or keep
the area warm. Until then
you've just got to face it.
Dr Grimgrave

SWOLLEN GLANDS

Dear Doc,
Thanks for your advice. I rested for two
weeks and I feel a lot better – my
appetite is back and I'm eating like a horse!
Fay C. Ake

Dear Ms Ake,
Eating like a horse are
you? Well, you'll only
get indigestion if you
don't sit down and use
a knife and fork like
everybody else.
Dr Grimgrave

Dear Doc,
I'm feeling sick and
achy and feverish
and my back and
chest and forehead are covered
in itching pus-filled spots.
I. B. Spottie
PS Sorry about the stains on
this letter.

124

> **Dear Mr Spottie,**
> You have chicken pox. It's a common virus and easy for an experienced doctor like me to spot. The best thing to do is rest and wait for the spots to become scabs and dry out. Don't bring them to me – I already have some in my collection. And don't pick them or they'll scar. At least you won't get chicken pox again, because your body will be immune to the virus.
> Goodbye!

Don't pick them!

Mind you, in the next chapter there's a virus so vicious and so nasty it'll make you *long* for chicken pox. Are you brave enough to read on … or are you about to turn chicken?

CLUCK! CLUCK!

YELLOW DEATH

There are over 150 names for yellow fever and some of them aren't very nice. For instance, you could call it "yellow breeze" or "yellow jack" or (just so long as it isn't a mealtime) "black vomit".

Bet you never knew!
In Jamaica in 1740 Dr John Williams announced yellow fever was different to blackwater fever. This is a fever (surprise, surprise) in which your pee turns brown or red (but not usually black). Local doctor Parker Bennett disagreed and challenged Williams to a duel. In the fight both doctors were killed.

YELLOW FEVER IS DEADLY...

BANG!

BANG!

IT SURE IS!

SCIENTIFIC NOTE

Williams was dead, but he was dead right. Blackwater fever is actually caused by another disease, malaria, attacking the kidneys (see page 152). The pee gets its colour from blood. Mind you, yellow fever is even worse! Would you care for a dose? Could it be worth it to get off school? ...

126

SICKENING SICK NOTE 3: YELLOW FEVER

Dear teacher,

I'm so worried about ~~me~~ ....
~~I'm~~ s/he's bright yellow! First s/he
had a flushed face, fever and aching.
And now the poor dear is in terrible
pain and bringing up black vomit and
bleeding from the ears and nose. The
doctor says it's yellow fever and I'm
at the end of my tether – I'm so
scared! So please excuse ~~me~~ her/him
for not doing any homework.

Signed,

An extremely concerned parent

blood →

Sick

Sickening sick note notes

1 The black colour is congealed blood.

2 The disease is spread by the aedes (a-ee-dez) mosquito. We trapped one of the little villains and extracted a confession…

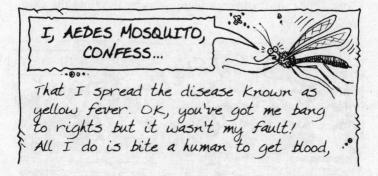

I, AEDES MOSQUITO, CONFESS...

That I spread the disease known as
yellow fever. OK, you've got me bang
to rights but it wasn't my fault!
All I do is bite a human to get blood,

I mean, I'm a mosquito right - that's me job. I only take a drop and don't mean no harm. I'm usually around at dusk if anyone wants to donate blood. It's not my fault if the blood sometimes has the virus that causes yellow fever. I mean, how am I supposed to know? It's not as if the victim is bright yellow! Well, OK they are - but I'm hungry. So I bite another victim and they get sick. Well, that's sad. You're not going to squash me, are you? Are you?

If the yellow fever virus could be caught and put on trial for crimes against humanity here is what the charge sheet might have said.

CHARGES AGAINST THE YELLOW FEVER VIRUS

1 That on or about the seventeenth century you crossed the Atlantic from Africa inside mosquitoes in ships bound for America. That you infected the sailors so that sometimes most of them were dead by the time the ship reached land.

2 That once in South America you killed off millions of innocent monkeys that had no immunity to you.

3 That you caused deadly epidemics in the Americas, Caribbean and even parts of Europe. For example, in 1802 you killed 23,000 French troops in Haiti and in 1821 you killed one in six people in Barcelona, Spain.

4 You caused such terror that in the 1840s the people of Memphis, USA considered abandoning their fever-ridden city and burning it to the ground.

DAFT DOCTORS

1 As usual, the doctors were confused about yellow fever. To begin with they thought it was caused by – surprise, surprise – bad smells.

In the 1790s in Philadelphia, a city ravaged every year by the disease, Dr Benjamin Rush blamed rotting coffee beans in the docks. But this theory wasn't worth a bean.

2 A certain Dr Firth was so sure that the disease couldn't be caught like flu he actually *drank* the disgusting black vomit made by a sufferer and *injected* himself with the victim's blood. Although by rights he should have got the disease, it didn't actually develop – perhaps because the virus was weak. Still, don't try this at home.

But scientists were closing in on the yellow fever and in 1900 George M Sternberg (of the US army) sent an elite team of scientists to Cuba to investigate the disease. Would they succeed when so many had failed? They were led by army doctor, Walter Reed. Here's what his reports to Sternberg might have looked like...

FOUR AGAINST THE YELLOW DEATH

Havana ~ June 1900

Dear George

I've just met the others for a chat.

A.A.

There's Aristides Agramonte - he's from round here and an expert on yellow fever - in fact he's been studying it for two years!

J.C.

James Carroll was born in England but as you know he's been in the US army for years. He's quiet and hard-working.

J.L.

Then there's Jesse Lazear, a pal of Agramonte. He's a bit posh but deep down he's a friendly guy.

W.R.

Oh and me, Walter Reed, the leader. We're getting on fine.

Well, let's hope we can find the cause of yellow fever. At present we HAVANA clue - geddit? First thing we're going to do is check out this guy Carlos Finlay. He's a local doctor who reckons the disease is spread by infected mosquitoes, but he can't prove it.

Kind regards, Walter

C.F.

July 1900

Dear George,

Strange things are happening at the army base. A soldier died of yellow fever whilst locked in the guard house. But the other prisoners didn't get the disease. Some soldiers have slept in the beds of yellow fever victims, complete with dried sick and poo on the sheets (soldiers ain't too fussy). But they didn't get the disease either! Blistering bedpans! Know what I'm thinking? I figure you can't get yellow fever by person-to-person - or even person-to-body-waste contact like an ordinary disease.

So maybe Finlay's right and it's something to do with them pesky mosquitoes? Jesse Lazear's been catching mosquitoes and letting them bite volunteers but so far no one has gone down with yellow fever - BLAST!

I'll keep you posted,   Walter

September 1900

Dear George,

As you know I'm back in the States but I've kept in touch with the others and can report a success - sort of.

Carroll and Lazear were in the lab and Jesse was showing off how to get a mosquito to bite a person.

"Don't think this one's hungry," said Lazear.

131

"Maybe it'll take a bite of me?" said Carroll, and sure enough it did. Well, shiver my stethoscope! Blow me if Carroll's not got yellow fever!

Mind you, I shouldn't joke - he could die.

Well, we've got to try this experiment again. We've still got the mosquito and its little tummy is rumbling. Luckily, there's a very stupid soldier at the base called William Dean and he's volunteered to be bitten!

CHOMP!

Derrr

Five days later...
I've just heard Dean's got yellow fever! He says it must have been something he ate! That proves the mosquito spreads yellow fever. Success at last!

Walter

DEADLY DISCOVERIES

1 The scientists had proved the mosquito spread yellow fever but fate was to play a cruel trick. A few days later Lazear was also bitten (quite by accident) and although Carroll and Dean survived the disease, Lazear did not. Sadly, he was not the only scientist to be killed by this deadly disease.

2 Japanese scientist Hideyo Noguchi (1876–1928) was already a famous and successful germ hunter when he decided that yellow fever was caused by bacteria. Sadly he was wrong – the disease is caused by a virus. In 1928 Hideyo was studying yellow fever in Africa when he died ... of yellow fever. His last words were "I don't understand." Too true – he didn't.

3 In 1927 Irish doctor Adrian Stokes (1887–1927) was in Africa trying to prove a link between yellow fever and monkeys when he caught the virus. He continued to experiment on monkeys using himself as a guinea pig, and proved that mosquitoes can pass the disease between monkeys and humans. Then he died.

4 Scientists didn't develop a vaccine to yellow fever until 1936. In that year a virus taken from a young African called Asibi was shown to be weakened so much that it no longer caused disease, but it made the body develop immunity. Since then the vaccine made from Asibi's virus has saved millions of lives.

GALLOPING GORGAS

Armed with the vital information that the aedes mosquito spreads yellow fever, scientists set about attacking the new enemy. None was more determined than US Major Walter Gorgas. With him it was all kind of *personal*.

When Gorgas had been a young officer his Colonel's daughter fell ill with yellow fever and the Colonel ordered Gorgas to speak at the girl's funeral. In fact, she recovered but Gorgas got the disease and the girl nursed him. They fell in love and got married.

In the 1880s a French attempt to build a canal across the Isthmus of Panama (the narrow bit between North and South America) failed when 52,816 labourers got yellow fever. In 1904 the Americans decided to have a go…

In 1904 Gorgas, by then a top army doctor, was ordered to Panama by the President to beat yellow fever. Gorgas sent thousands of men into the battle. He wanted oil poured on all open water so the mosquito couldn't lay eggs and bushes burnt so that the mosquito couldn't hide.

Gorgas had to face opposition from his bosses in the US Army.

Colonel Goethals complained:

By 1906 Panama was free of yellow fever and the canal was completed in 1913. For the first time ever, humans had taken on a deadly disease on its own ground … and won!

Bet you never knew!
Today, yellow fever is still lurking in the tropics (the warm regions of the world) but it's no longer a massive killer. That's the good news – but one of its revolting relatives, dengue fever, is spreading. This disease is also spread by aedes mosquitoes and it's known as "breakbone fever" because it feels like all your bones and joints are breaking apart. Fancy a break off school, then?

SOME GOOD NEWS AT LAST...

It's typical. Just when we think we're beating a disease another one pops up. It's a bit worrying, isn't it? Well, here's a bit of good news. There's one deadly disease that we've beaten fair and square – for *ever*!

You'll find the next chapter a real shot in the arm...

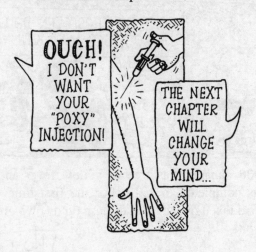

SMALLPOX SMASHED

For thousands of years a war has been raging between microbes and humans. It's a war without mercy on either side, and millions of humans and trillions of germs have died. But at last, after thousands of years of sickness and suffering, humans won a great victory – over smallpox. So what was this deadly disease like?

If you've ever had measles then you'll know what *that's* like. Can you imagine measles ONE HUNDRED times as bad? If not, you'd better read this…

SICKENING SICK NOTES 4: SMALLPOX

Dear teacher,

I don't know what to do! The doctor says my poor .... has smallpox! It began with a violent raging fever and throwing up and agonizing muscle pains from head to toe and later a horrible rash. Now the fever is worse and the rash is a mass of huge pus-filled spots! Germs have attacked the spots and ~~my~~ his/her skin is rotting and falling off! I can't stand it and nor can poor .... Please excuse ~~me~~ him/her from all science lessons – *for ever!*

Signed,

Very worried parent

Sickening sick note notes

1 Like measles, smallpox is caused by a virus. The brick-shaped smallpox virus is called variola.

2 The virus can be spread by touching the scabs and by infected breath. If there was an outbreak of smallpox at your school they'd have to close down the whole school for months.

3 Unfortunately, I mean luckily, no one gets smallpox any more (for reasons you're about to discover) so your teacher might not believe your sick note and then she might realize that all the others were made up too.

THIS IS YOUR DEATH!

In its time smallpox killed millions of people. I wonder what the *This Is Your Death* people would make of it?

WELCOME TO THE TV PROGRAMME THAT PUTS THE LIFE BACK INTO DEATH.

Today we're at a high security laboratory to meet a celebrity who has touched the hearts of people around the world – and other parts of their bodies too. We've shrunk down to interview the smallpox virus – Variola major, this is your death!

THIS IS YOUR DEATH!

Wow! I don't get too many visitors here!

No one knows where you came from. But in your time you've been very close to royalty. Indeed, it's said you made a killing from your connections with them. Here are your royal chums... Come in Your Majesties!

I sure did.

GRRR!

Ramases V of Egypt (died 1157 BC), Mary II of England (died 1694), Peter II of Russia (died 1730) and Louis XV of France (died 1774).

Luis I of Spain (died 1742), two Emperors of Japan (both died 548) and the Inca Emperor Huayna-Capac (died 1526).

Er – nice to see you again guys.

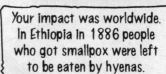

Numerous people were left scarred by your scabs, including George Washington.

Yes, I've left my mark on history.

Your impact was worldwide. In Ethiopia in 1886 people who got smallpox were left to be eaten by hyenas.

GRRR!

I've always had a soft spot for animals!

SINISTER SMALLPOX STORIES

One of the first to study smallpox was Arab doctor, Abu Bakr Mohammed ibn Zakaria (860–932), known as al-Rhazes, who described the differences between smallpox and measles on the basis of observing the sufferers. Just in case you're wondering…

1 Measles makes you sneeze in the early stages and this gives you a red nose.

AS YOU CAN SEE, THIS MAN IS DELIGHTED THAT HE HASN'T GOT SMALLPOX

2 Measles spots are smaller than smallpox spots and don't form scabs.

3 With measles you also get white spots in the mouth.

Rhazes wrote 200 books, mostly about philosophy and religion – but his religious views fell foul of a powerful mullah (Islamic priest). The mullah ordered Rhazes to be beaten with his own book until either the book broke or his head broke.

CLONK!

OUCH! I WISH WE'D ONLY PRINTED PAPERBACKS

Unfortunately, Rhazes' head wasn't as thick as his book and he got brain damage and went blind.

SMALLPOX GOES WEST

When smallpox arrived in America in 1521 it triggered the greatest disaster in human history, something that made the Black Death look like the Teddy Bear's Picnic. The disease was brought over by Europeans. Many Europeans had had the disease and their bodies were immune to it but the native Americans had never encountered smallpox (or other European diseases such as measles and flu) and so they had no protection.

And they had no more idea of how to cure the disease than the Europeans. The native treatment, sweating the disease out and then jumping into icy water, only hastened death. (Mind you, some schools still practise this technique – it's known as the "swimming lesson".)

For over 200 years smallpox happily rampaged through the Americas like a caterpillar in a cabbage patch. In all, one hundred *million* people may have died.

The defeat of smallpox began with a custom that developed separately in China and Turkey. It was called inoculation and it involved giving a person a mild dose of the disease to boost their immunity. It's a bit like vaccination, but this time the virus is alive. A remarkable woman worked to spread the custom around the world...

Hall of fame: Mary Wortley Montague (1689–1762) Nationality: British

Mary had every reason to hate smallpox. She was a beautiful and talented young woman of 26 when the disease struck. And it left horrific scars on her face. Before then her dad had tried to marry her off to an incredibly boring man named Clotworthy. (I didn't make that bit up, honest!) When Mary refused, her dad locked her in the house and got her sister to spy on her. (Little sisters can be vicious…)

Anyway, Mary escaped with her rich pompous boyfriend, Edward Montague, who became ambassador to Turkey.

And it was there that Mary came across inoculation. Here's what she might have written to her friend, Sarah Chiswell, in England…

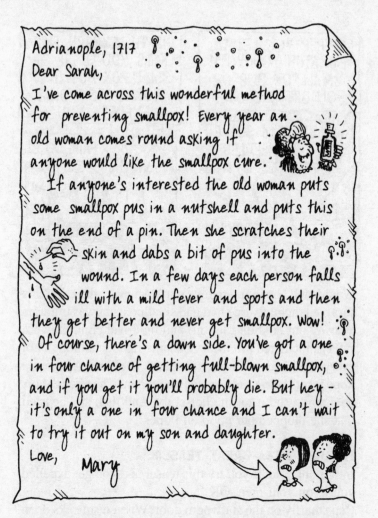

Adrianople, 1717
Dear Sarah,
I've come across this wonderful method for preventing smallpox! Every year an old woman comes round asking if anyone would like the smallpox cure.

If anyone's interested the old woman puts some smallpox pus in a nutshell and puts this on the end of a pin. Then she scratches their skin and dabs a bit of pus into the wound. In a few days each person falls ill with a mild fever and spots and then they get better and never get smallpox. Wow! Of course, there's a down side. You've got a one in four chance of getting full-blown smallpox, and if you get it you'll probably die. But hey – it's only a one in four chance and I can't wait to try it out on my son and daughter.
Love,
Mary

Mary's children survived. Back in England in 1718, Lady Mary suggested the treatment for the daughters of her friend the Princess of Wales. The Princess wasn't so sure so Mary suggested a horrifying experiment. Six criminals awaiting execution were given a deadly choice…

143

Would YOU be dying to take part? Anyway, the criminals survived (actually one had had smallpox and was immune anyway but he didn't let on) and the royal children were safely inoculated too. Mary became famous although not everyone liked her bossy manner. The poet Alexander Pope wrote some rude verses about her so she bought his book and used it to line her potty. And then she boasted that she plopped her poop on Pope.

TEACHER'S TEA-BREAK TEASER

Important note: if you try this teaser and you get expelled you're on your own, OK.

Rap smartly on the staffroom door. When it squeaks open give your teacher a sunny smile and enquire:

144

Answer: Yes, your teacher might have a scar (usually about 1 cm across) on her upper arm where she was vaccinated as a baby. All children were vaccinated before 1976 so this is a good way of finding out if your teacher is as young as she claims to be.

SMALLPOX GOES WEST (AND THIS TIME FOR GOOD)

In 1796, Jenner developed cowpox vaccinations to fight smallpox (remember that bit from page 57). So it was now possible to stop people getting smallpox. And unlike plague the disease didn't hide in wild animals and unlike yellow fever it wasn't spread by insects. The virus only lived in people and if everyone was vaccinated then the virus would die out. In 1966, following a suggestion by Russian scientists, the World Health Organization set out to do just that.

Led by US doctor Donald Henderson, 650 WHO health-workers scoured the world for smallpox. In Brazil a doctor was kidnapped but before he was released he insisted on vaccinating his captors against the disease.

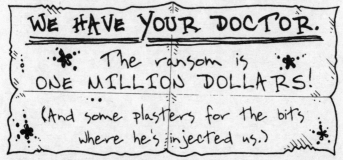

Another doctor was killed by a native American arrow. Eventually the disease was found only in Somalia and Bangladesh and then in 1980 there came the long-awaited announcement. Smallpox had been wiped off

145

the face of the Earth (though a few samples were kept for research). For the first time in millions of years humans had destroyed a deadly disease!

Well, that was the good news. But meanwhile new deadly diseases were appearing – but where were they coming from? And why did they have to be so *nasty*? Are they really out to get us? Read on and find out...

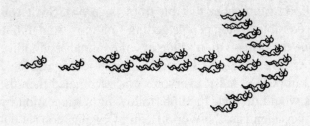

NASTY NEWCOMERS

I'm afraid the facts about some of these new diseases make rather miserable reading. Dr Grimgrave is happily putting together a dossier on some of the worst offenders…

HORRIBLE HEALTH WARNING!

READERS MAY LIKE TO PUT A HANKIE OVER THEIR NOSE AND MOUTH AT THIS POINT. YOU DON'T WANT TO RISK CATCHING ANYTHING NASTY, DO YOU?

ROGUE'S GALLERY

WANTED FOR MURDER

BACTERIAL DISEASES

LEGIONNAIRE'S DISEASE

<u>First known appearance:</u> Philadelphia, USA, 1976.

<u>Known crimes:</u> Killed former members of the American Legion staying at a hotel. Since then has appeared all over the world. I would

A NOTE FROM DR GRIMGRAVE I object to the light-hearted presentation of serious factual information. Anyone would think that this book is a publication of a humorous nature.

like to study it further but
unfortunately none of my patients
has caught it.

Method of operation: Attacks the
lungs and causes fever.

Known associates: Lives
inside a protozoan that
lives in shower heads and
air-conditioning systems.

Danger rating: Still rare
and can be treated with
antibiotics.

LYME DISEASE

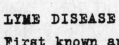

First known appearance:
Studied by scientists at
Old Lyme, Connecticut,
USA 1975.

Known crimes: Attacked a group of
children in the town, they all
recovered. Since then has appeared
all over the USA and parts of
Europe, China, Japan and South Africa.

Method of operation: My colleague Dr
Gripe got this illness and it caused
him a few gripes I can tell you. He
suffered fever, rash, stiff neck,
aching joints and years of pain. But
luckily he was a patient patient.

TICK

Known associates: Lives
inside tiny biting bugs
such as deer ticks. The tick
collects the virus by biting
mice and can pass it on to
humans by biting them.

Danger rating: Not fatal – can be treated with antibiotics.

HUMOROUS NOTE
Teachers must be a health hazard because they're always giving you ticks. Sorry, Dr G!

VIRUSES

EBOLA

First known appearance: Sudan and Congo Republic, Africa, 1976.

Known crimes: Kills between 50 and 80 per cent of victims.

Method of operation: Spread by contact with body fluids such as blood and vomit. Symptoms include violent headaches, bleeding from the ears, eyeballs and bottom. Hair and fingernails drop off. Certainly a fascinating disease, I watched a programme about the symptoms whilst eating supper last night.

Known associates: None.

Danger rating: Very rare even in Africa. All outbreaks have been contained.

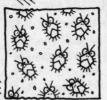

AIDS

First known appearance:
Africa, probably in the
1950s. There are actually
several varieties of the
HIV virus (Human Immuno-
deficiency Virus) that cause the
disease known as AIDS (Acquired
Immune Deficiency Syndrome).

Known crimes: If left untreated, kills
99.9 per cent of all its victims.

Method of operation:
1 Hides inside the DNA
of the T-cells where
it's impossible for
the immune system to
find it.

Horribly complicated
– to get your head
round it you might
like to check back to
page 111.

2 After several months or
even years, for unknown reasons, the
virus starts to attack more T-cells.

Basically what happens is that the
virus kills more and more T-cells
until the immune system can't fight
off germs such as TB bacteria.

Known associates: It's these other
deadly diseases that actually kill
the patient.

Danger rating: Deadly, but because
the virus is spread by contact with
body fluids such as blood, it's
quite hard to get. You can't get it
from someone coughing over you or
even from sharing a toothbrush or a
toilet with a sufferer, like some
idiots claim.

SO WHY ARE WE GETTING ALL THESE NEW DISEASES?

Ask two scientists and you'll be given three different answers (at least).

THE CLIMATE IS GETTING WARMER AND THIS MAKES IT EASIER FOR INSECTS THAT SPREAD DISEASE TO BREED.

AND AS PEOPLE TRAVEL MORE THEY TAKE GERMS WITH THEM. THIS MEANS THAT DISEASE CAN SPREAD FASTER.

AND DON'T FORGET MANY PEOPLE NOW LIVE CLOSE TOGETHER IN BIG CITIES WHERE DISEASES CAN SPREAD EASILY.

As usual with science there's no simple answer. But there's one explanation that many scientists support. Many of the new diseases are spread by animals. AIDS and ebola have been found in monkeys, Lyme disease is spread by ticks and so on. What seems to be happening is that as humans settle in wild areas of the world and cut down forests we pick up diseases that have existed there for thousands of years. That's probably how we first got the plague from the cute furry animals that normally carry it.

So it's all our fault? Charming!

Depressing reading, eh?

151

Well, cheer up – it gets worse. You know all those lovely diseases that we've been talking about and which you might have thought were beaten by modern medicine? Well, some old favourites have been crawling out of the dustbin of history. Take the lung disease TB…

TB: THE BAD NEWS…
To cure TB you take antibiotics for up to a year. But most people feel better after a few months and the drugs are expensive so it's easy to give up the treatment. This is a massive mistake because it means that the remaining TB germs are the strongest and the most able to survive the drugs, and they can stage a comeback. In many parts of the world TB is now resistant to antibiotics. So today millions of children need to be tested for TB. (If you're a budding actor you could say "TB or not TB, that is the question.")

MALARIA: MORE BAD NEWS
In Africa, 3,000 people die of malaria every day and it's getting worse. It's reckoned that a person gets bitten by an infected mosquito every *30 seconds*. (That person must be getting sick of it by now! Sorry, sick joke.)

In many parts of the world the mosquitoes that carry the disease can't be killed by sprays. The reason is the

152

same as for the TB germs: the mosquitoes' bodies have learnt to deal with the poisons. And the protozoa that cause the disease are increasingly able to survive anti-malaria drugs.

Here's something to take your mind off it...

COULD YOU BE A DOCTOR?

You're in Dr Grimgrave's waiting room. You've got a splinter in your little finger. (Let's hope he's in a good mood and doesn't cut it off!) The other patients aren't in the pink of health. Can you work out what's wrong with them...?

CLUE: Try looking back at the diseases mentioned in this book.

1 SKIN IS PURPLE-BLUE. JUST ABOUT TO DASH TO THE TOILET.

2 LICE. SPLITTING HEADACHE AND FEVER. RASH.

3 BRIGHT YELLOW SKIN. VIOLENT FEVER. BOWL OF BLACK SICK.

4 SWOLLEN FACE. FEELING SICK.

NEXT!

SOME GOOD NEWS AT LONG LAST!

Science *is* fighting back… Here's an exclusive peek at some of the latest high-tech drugs that are heading our way. Yes, here in one of Dr Grimgrave's medical magazines!

MEDICAL NEWS

NEW DRUG BREAKTHROUGHS!

RESISTANT BACTERIA

ANTIBIOTIC PROBLEMS

Scientists are always working to develop new drugs. This week we report on the latest developments...

Amazing antibiotics

When bacteria have become resistant to an antibiotic scientists want to know why. It's usually because the bacteria make a chemical that sticks to the antibiotic and stops it working. As one drug company representative said: "It's a real sticky problem." One response is to add a chemical to the antibiotic that sticks to the bacteria chemical and stops *it* working.

Designer DNA

Scientists are trying to attack the DNA in a virus.

That's the chemical that controls how the virus develops (some viruses use a simpler chemical called RNA but the effect is the same).

The idea is to make a protein chemical that can stick to the DNA and stop it working. This stops the virus from multiplying.

Argh! My DNA's stopped working!

WANTED FOR MEDICAL COLLECTION

Dead body parts showing signs of unusual disease. Rare pustules, blisters and sores particularly welcome.
Contact:
Dr Grimgrave,
The Surgery,
Much Moaning.

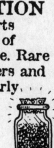

TRY NEW AMOXYCILLIN

(on your patients that is!).
This antibiotic stops bacteria from making cell walls, so that water can flow into them until they go pop. Now with improved chemicals to stop the bacteria getting rid of the antibiotic before it kills them!

BRAND-NEW BREAKTHROUGHS!

Thanks to genetic engineering we can make bacteria produce large amounts of vital chemicals such as antitoxins or interferon. (As all readers know, interferon is the vital substance that stops viruses multiplying.) Another area of research is artificial antibodies called monoclonal antibodies. Grown in cells kept in laboratories, these chemicals can be used like antibodies to block toxins.

My monoclonal antibodies are growing well, this year

Next week

▷ Would we doctors be happier without patients?

▷ Fascinating gory operations in full colour.

▷ Our "long-running" series on body fluids features an in-depth report on diarrhoea and vomit.

WARNING!
The next bit won't just scare the socks off you – it might scare your toe nails off too!

Bet you never knew!
Have you ever had a really bad nightmare? Well, if you're a virologist chances are your worst nightmare would be about H5N1. It's a kind of flu that bumps off birds in huge numbers. But the scary thing is that it could change its DNA and do the same thing to us. It would be like 1918 all over again only even more nasty. Whenever the virus appears scientists try to kill all the birdlife to stop it spreading. In 1997 they killed all the chickens in Hong Kong. So far the virus hasn't spread widely amongst people. We've been lucky ... so far.

But will the next time be the *last time*? Perhaps, lurking somewhere out there is a germ so nasty, so vicious that it could wipe out life on this planet! Better read on and find out!

EPILOGUE:
A SICKENING FUTURE?

So will a new disease appear and wipe us out?

The answer's no so please DON'T PANIC!

Even if there were such a disease (and some diseases are pretty anti-social as you've just found out), it's *not* going to destroy us and here's why. Doctors now have the knowledge and the technology to keep people healthier than they've ever been before.

YOU'RE LATE FOR YOUR CHECKUP, MRS WHEELER!

SORRY DOC, MY MOUNTAIN BIKE GOT A PUNCTURE COMING DOWN CRAGGY FELL

You can shiver at deadly diseases but you don't have to be scared of them. Most can be cured if treated quickly.

So even if a new deadly disease appears we know enough about diseases to ensure that it won't keep spreading. We know about techniques such as vaccination and antibiotics that can fight it. The truth is that although the battle against deadly diseases hasn't been won altogether – we're still gaining ground.

And there's more. For a disease to wipe us out it would have to kill us before scientists could devise any kind of treatment. Of course a few diseases *do* kill quickly – think of the 1918 influenza. But most diseases aren't that rapid – for a horribly good reason. If people died in five minutes then the germs would be buried with their first victim and never spread. And being buried alive is a nasty fate – even for a germ.

But if the disease spreads over a period of months and years then there would be time for some people to come into contact with just a few germs and get a mild dose of the disease. These people would fall ill and recover and so develop immunity.

And there's an even better reason why we should be OK. *Human nature.*

This has been a book about death and suffering and pain. But in the worst times you can sometimes glimpse the best in people. People like the scientists who risk their lives and sometimes die to conquer a particular deadly disease. Or the volunteers who agree to take part in experiments that might leave them sick or dying.

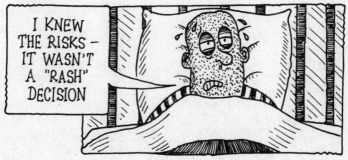

Or the doctors who work round the clock to keep their patients alive, or Gunnar Kaasen and the other sledge drivers who raced to save children from diphtheria.

Ultimately, people try to help one another. It's the best way for us all to survive, and it's the reason why, whatever happens, humans will continue to fight and win the battle against deadly diseases. And that's the not-so-horrible truth!

DEADLY DISEASES

QUIZ

Now find out if you're a
Deadly Diseases expert!

Ghastly germs and vampire viruses

You carry germs around with you every day, but how much do you really know about them? Try these true or false questions to see if you're a germ genius or a disease dunce.

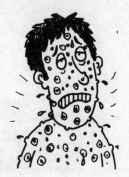

1 Germs are carried on bad smells. True or false?

2 A fever is the body's way of heating up germs so much that they die. True or false?

3 Interferon is a chemical that stops viruses from multiplying. True or false?

4 Once you've had a disease caused by a bacteria or a virus you won't get it again. True or false?

5 Picking your nose and eating the snot helps build up antibodies that can prevent colds. True or false?

6 Viruses can be spread by simply shaking hands with an infected person. True or false?

7 Your nose runs when you have a cold because your body is trying to get rid of the cold germs. True or false?

8 A vaccine is actually a dose of a disease. True or false?

Answers:

1 False – germs are everywhere. It's more likely that they're the cause of bad smells than the result of them!

2 True – the fever heats the germs until they die.

3 True – the body produces interferon naturally, but stupid scientists don't know how!

4 True – the antigens stay in your body and will attack the disease if it comes back.

5 False – not only is picking your nose disgusting, it's also bad for you. The germs in the snot can get into your guts and give you a runny tummy.

6 False – viruses are spread through scratches in the skin or on tiny drops of spit like those that fly out of your granny's mouth when she's speaking.

7 True – your snot contains all the nasty stuff that your body is trying to get rid of.

8 True – but it's a very mild dose, just enough to get your body working to create the antigens to protect it from the disease in the future.

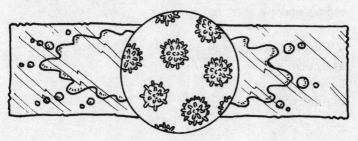

Battling body quiz

So, you think you've figured out the way your battling body works? Try these quick questions to see if you're fit to lead the charge against enemy invaders...

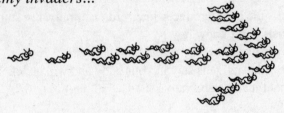

1 Where in the body are blood cells made?
a) Bone marrow
b) Snot
c) Intestines

2 What is a macrophage?
a) A type of computer program
b) A type of protein
c) A type of white blood cell

3 What is pus made of?
a) Dead bacteria and cells
b) Slugs and snails
c) Snot and mucus

4 What do scientists call invaders of the body?
a) Antibodies
b) Antigens
c) Antifreeze

5 Where won't you find germs?
a) In your baby brother's nappy
b) In your lunchbox
c) On the planet Mars

6 How often do bacteria split in half?
a) Every 20 minutes
b) Every three days
c) Every third Tuesday of the month

7 What type of enemy invaders can antibiotics cure?
a) Maggots
b) Viruses
c) Bacteria

8 What are rickettsia?
a) Germs that give you bendy bones and bandy legs.
b) Deadly disease bacteria that live inside cells.
c) Viruses shaped like TV aerials.

Answers:
1a; 2c; 3a; 4b; 5c; 6a; 7c; 8b

Shocking symptoms

Have you learned enough to be able to work out what icky illness someone has just by their symptoms? Look at the list below and match the symptoms to the deadly disease.

1 Violent coughing, boils on the skin
2 Fear of water, mad dribbling
3 Coughing blood, snotty phlegm
4 Sneezing, runny nose, sore throat
5 Oozing sore throat, sense of suffocating
6 Muscle pains, pus-filled spots on the skin
7 Fever, headache, vomiting, rash on the skin
8 Fever with cold sweats, muscle spasms

a) Tuberculosis
b) Diphtheria
c) Malaria
d) Plague
e) Smallpox
f) Rabies
g) Common cold
h) Meningitis

Answers:
1d; 2f; 3a; 4g; 5b; 6e; 7h; 8c

Crazy cures

It's not enough just to identify the disease, though – you have to cure them too. Look at the list of diseases below. Can you figure out what cures dastardly doctors came up with in the past?

1 Cholera
2 Diphtheria
3 Typhoid fever
4 Plague
5 Smallpox
6 Rabies
7 Common cold
8 Flu

a) Rub toad's blood all over your body
b) Burn the wound with a red-hot iron
c) Eat chicken soup
d) Sweat the disease out then jump into iced water
e) Cover the body with blood-sucking leeches
f) Drink poison
g) Drink brandy every hour
h) Shave your head

Answers:
1e; 2g; 3h; 4a; 5d; 6b; 7c; 8f

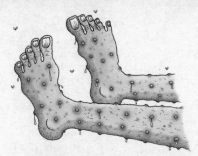

HORRIBLE INDEX

HORRIBLE SCIENCE

NASTY NATURE

I LOVE FAST FOOD!

NICK ARNOLD *illustrated by* **TONY DE SAULLES**

ISBN 978 0439 94451 9

HORRIBLE SCIENCE

DISGUSTING DIGESTION

IT TAKES GUTS!

NICK ARNOLD *illustrated by* **TONY DE SAULLES**

ISBN 978 0439 94445 8

HORRIBLE SCIENCE

UGLY BUGS

NOT A PRETTY SIGHT!

NICK ARNOLD *illustrated by* **TONY DE SAULLES**

ISBN 978 0439 94452 6

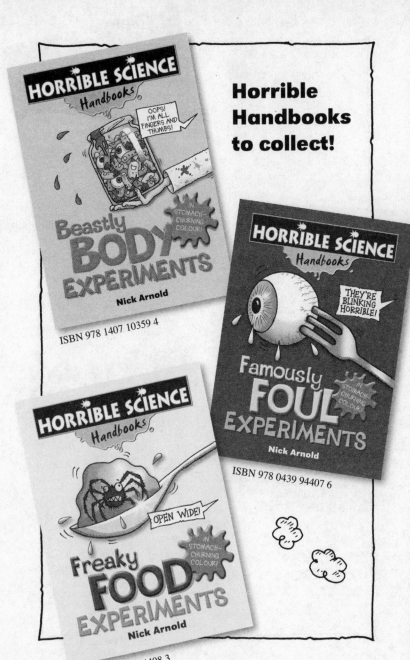

Horrible Handbooks to collect!